GUCCI

GUCCI.COM

**PRADA**

+44 207 309 2030 prada.com

PRADA

BRUCE WEBER

# LOUIS VUITTON

JUERGEN TELLER

# SERIES 2  A curated series of photography by
ANNIE LEIBOVITZ, JUERGEN TELLER and BRUCE WEBER

LOUIS VUITTON

# MIU MIU

STEVEN MEISEL
NEW YORK, NOVEMBER 22-24 2014
MARINE VACTH

miu miu

STEVEN MEISEL
NEW YORK, NOVEMBER 22-24 2014
MIA GOTH

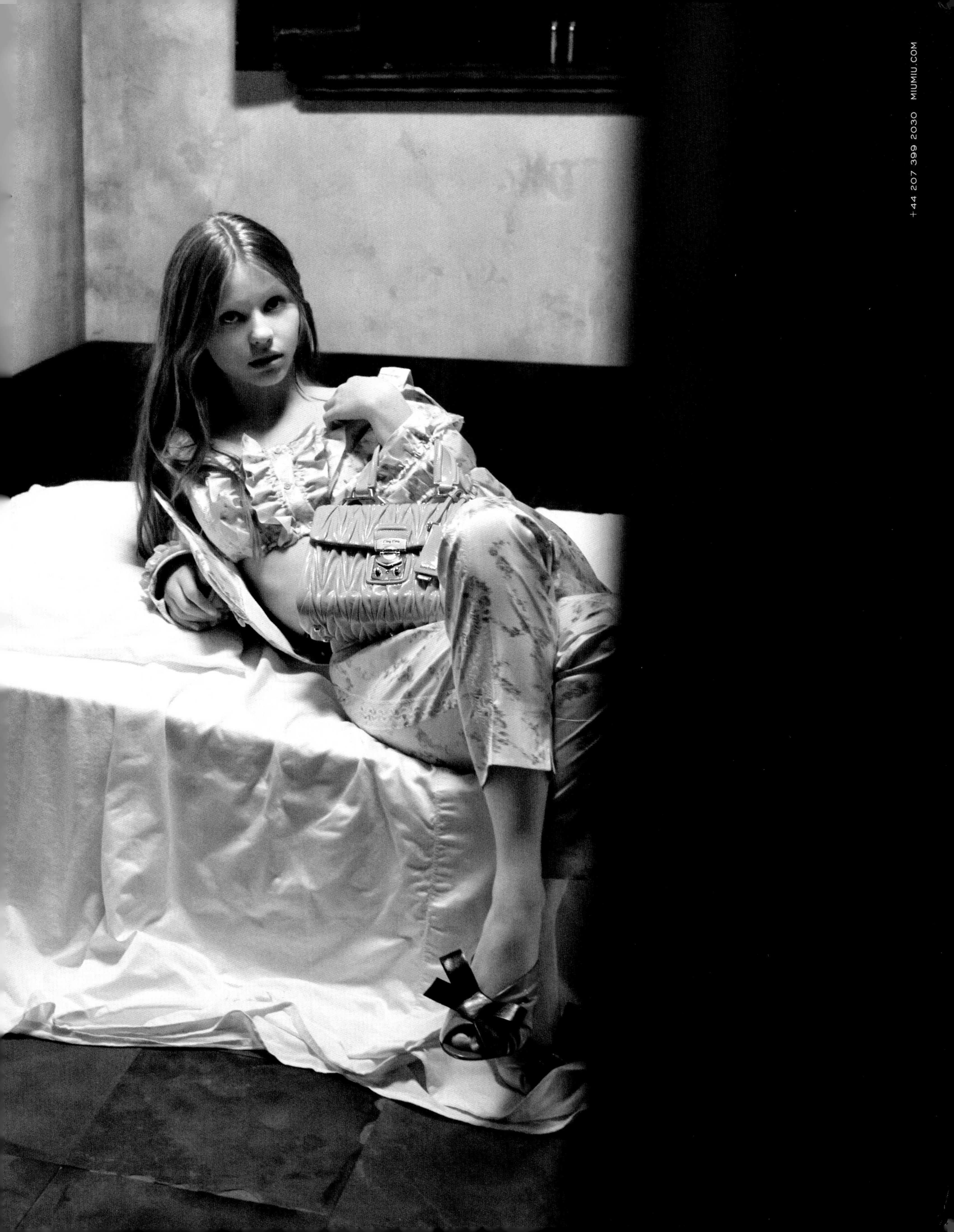
+44 207 399 2030 MIUMIU.COM

SAINT LAURENT

PARIS

**SAINT LAURENT**

PARIS

DIOR

HOMME

See the film
DIOR.COM/TheLetter

HOMME

See the film
DIOR.COM/TheLetter

BALEN

CIAGA

BALEN

rag &

# bone

NEW YORK

rag &

bone

NEW YORK

**SPRING 2015**
Edie in pale blue
Cropped Mod Jacket on Molly
Crosby Carryall in pale blue/teal
Wild Beast Short Peacoat on Valery
coach.com

# COACH
## NEW YORK

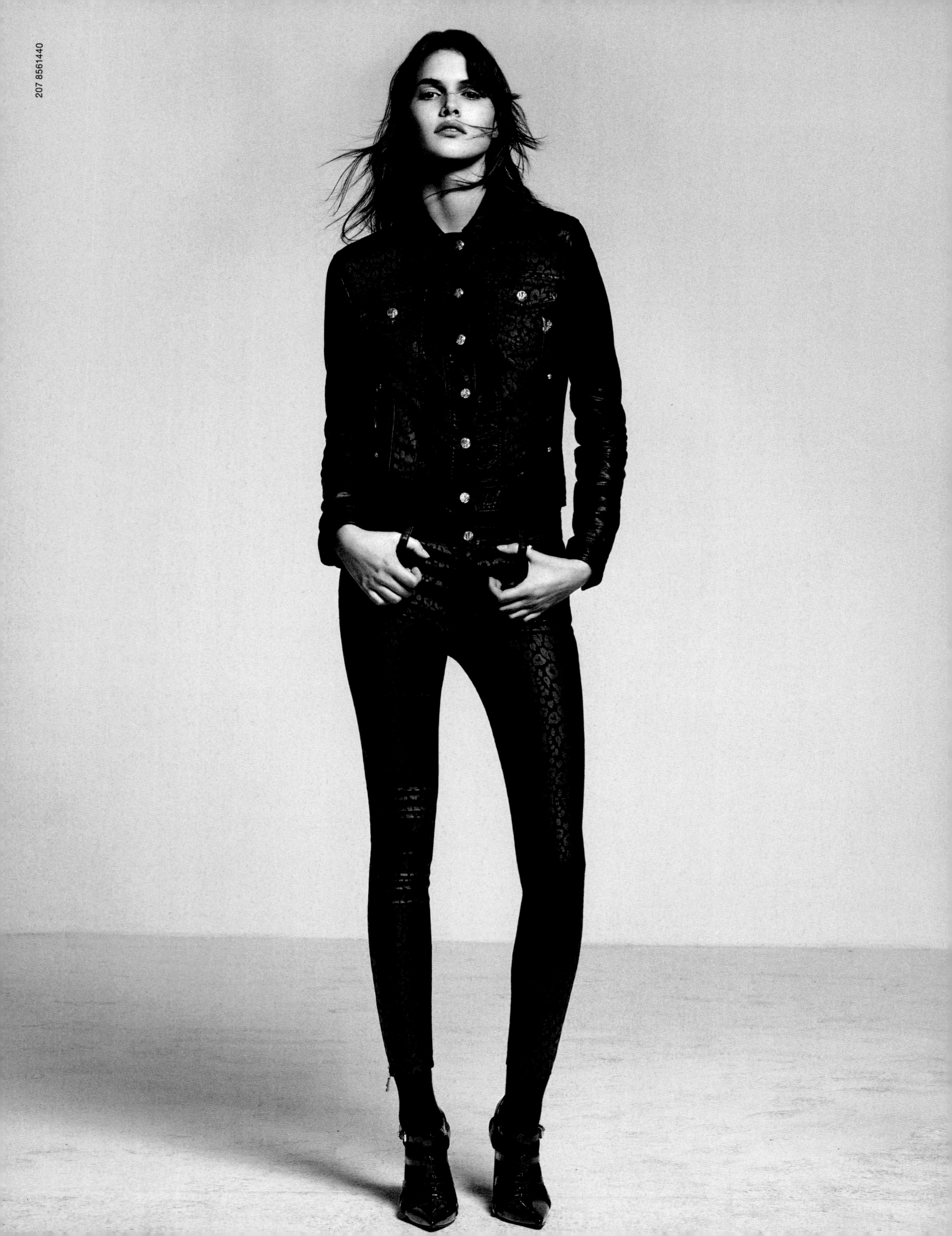
207 8561440

DKNY

# DSQUARED2

NEW FLAGSHIP STORE
51 CONDUIT STREET - LONDON

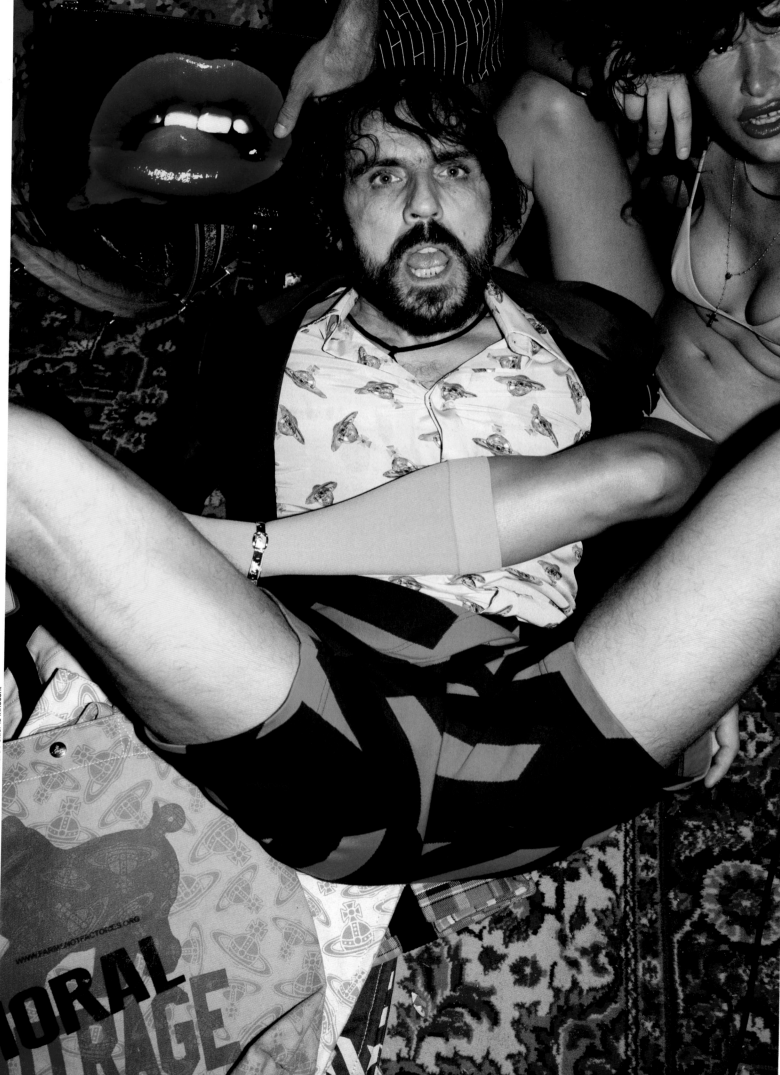

PAULSMITH.CO.UK

SONIA

RYKIEL

PARIS

ROMAN CLASSICISM
n.22 - ryan / karolin / rhys

neilbarrett.com

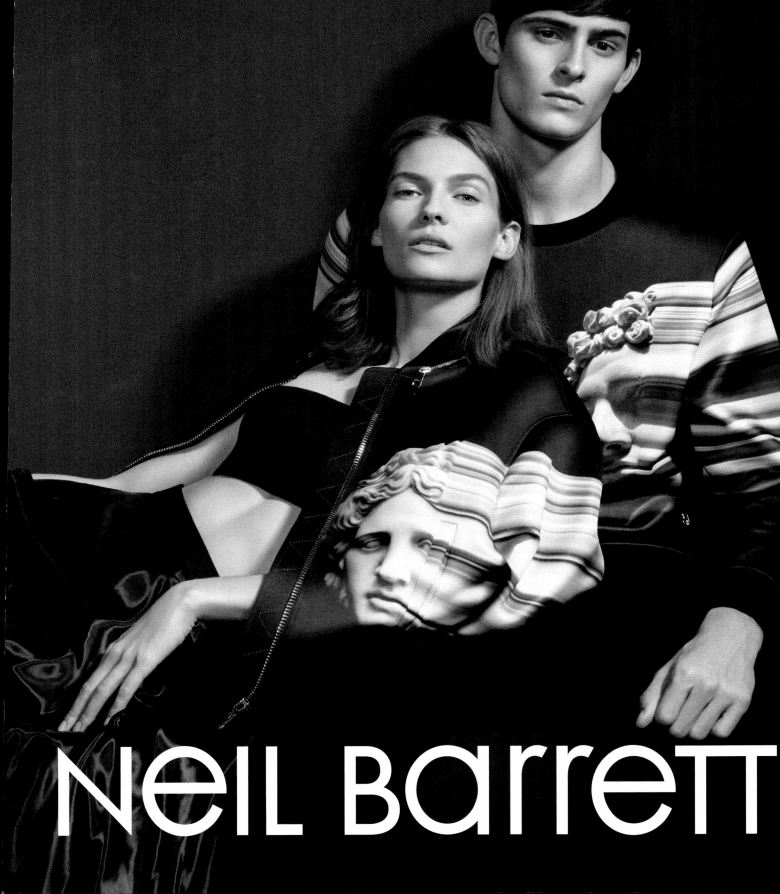

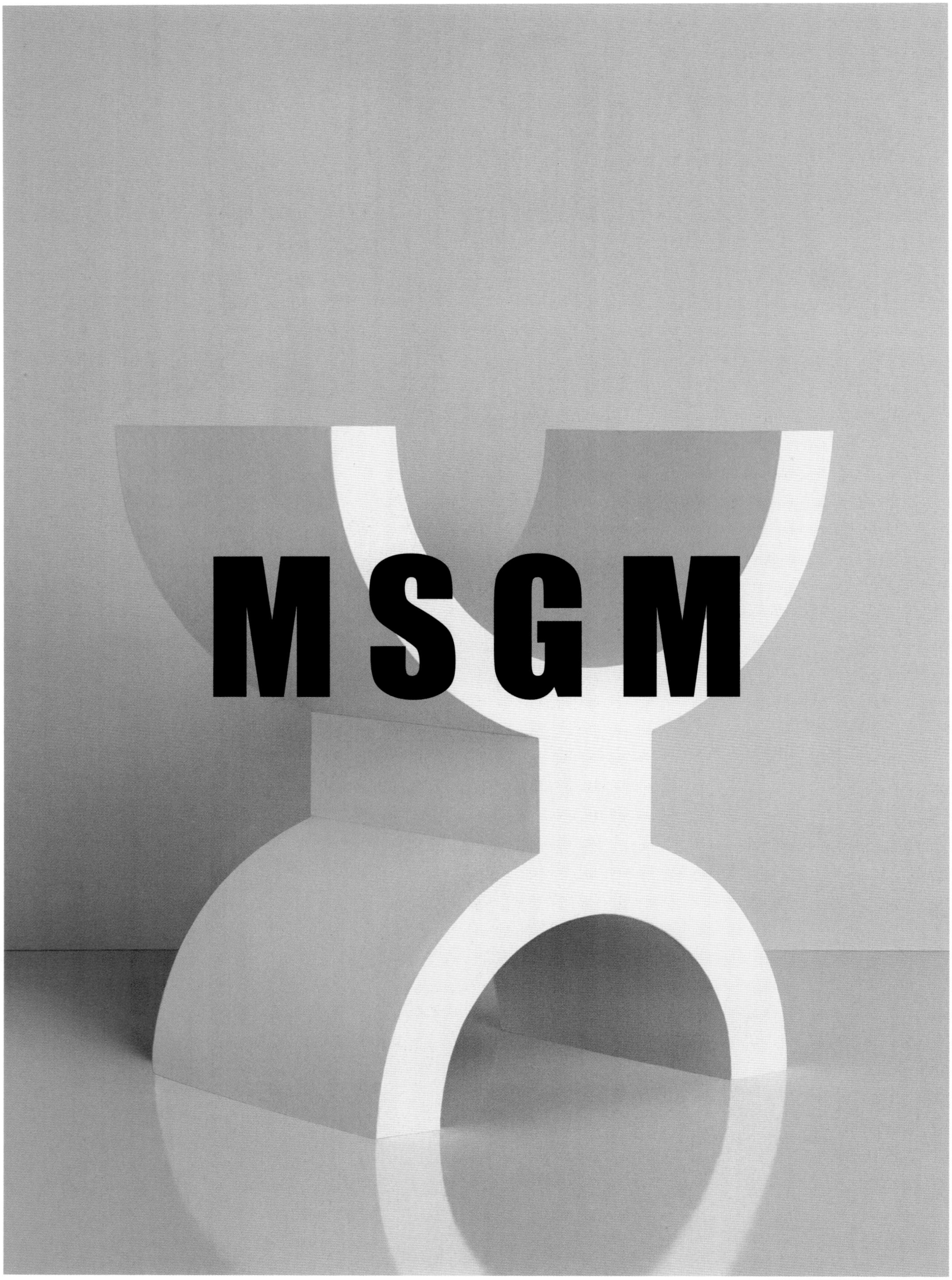
MSGM

byblos
MILANO

**PROUDLY MADE IN THE UK SINCE 1937**

Jacob Sutton, Restauranteur

#DIESELHIGH

TOPSHOP

# AVANT TOI
## 20th anniversary

**G-STAR RAW**

JEANS

photography by ellen von unwerth | g-star.com

ERIKA CAVALLINI

SEMICOUTURE

# Champions of Fashion.

The new Mercedes-AMG GT and Dree Hemingway with Lewis Hamilton and Nico Rosberg, captured by Collier Schorr. www.mercedes-benz.com/fashion

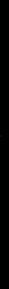

Fuel consumption combined: 9.6–9.3 l/100 km; combined $CO_2$ emissions: 224–216 g/km.

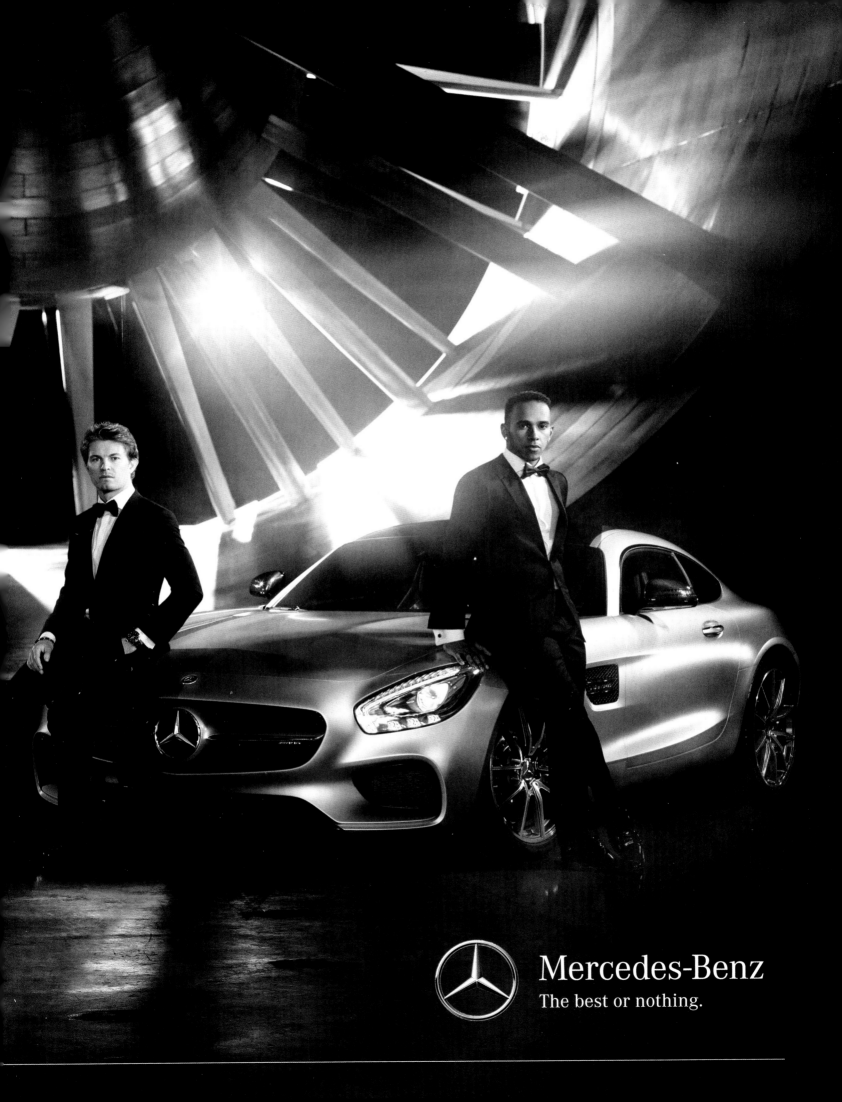

FIND YOUR 501® CT JEANS.
LEVI.COM

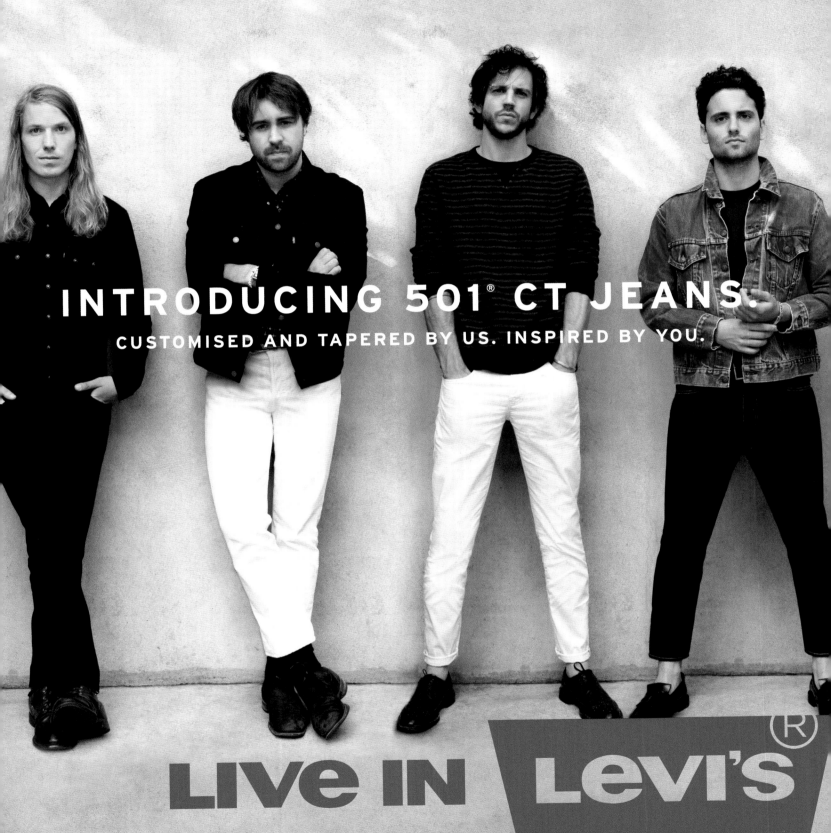

INTRODUCING 501® CT JEANS.
CUSTOMISED AND TAPERED BY US. INSPIRED BY YOU.

LIVE IN Levi's®

501® CT JEAN

WORN BY THE VACCINES

my
PET
& ME

LONDON
FASHION
WEEK

THE NEW COLLECTION 2015

swatch®⊞

Pepe Jeans®
LONDON
MADE FOR MISCHIEF

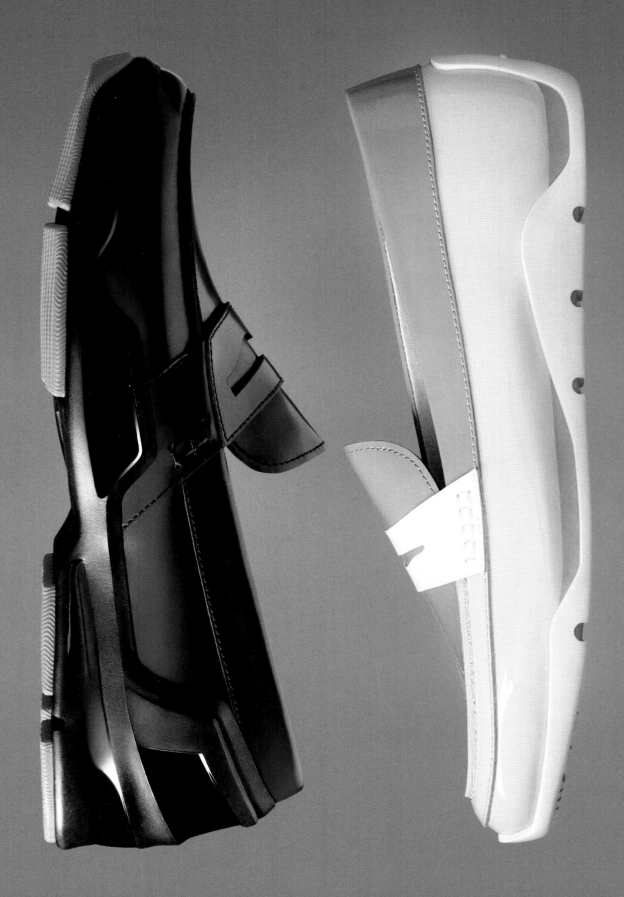

CAMPER

EVISU.COM

BE THE O

# Contents

## the cover

Yo-landi Visser wears
cotton jumpsuit by
Marc by Marc Jacobs

Photography
Pierre Debusschere
Styling
Robbie Spencer

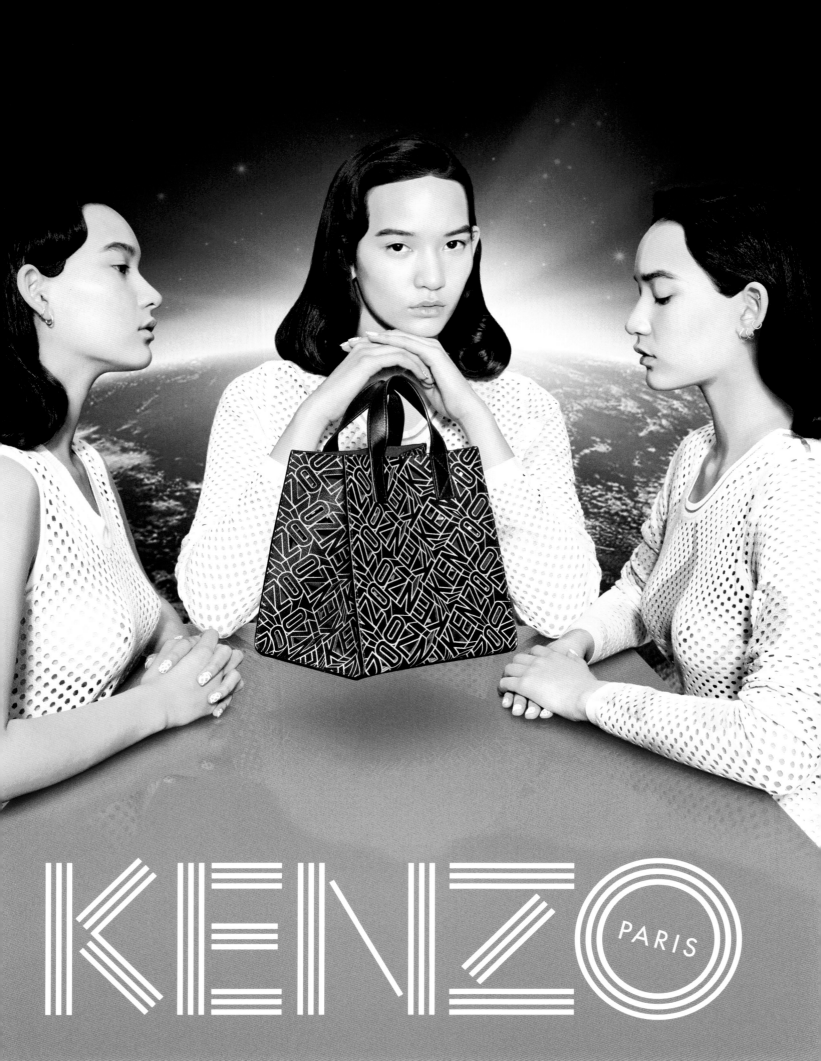

ILARIA NISTRI

## editorial

editor-in-chief
TIM NOAKES
tim@dazedgroup.com

editor
ISABELLA BURLEY
isabella@dazedgroup.com

digital editor
CHARLIE ROBIN JONES
charlie@dazedgroup.com

deputy editor
OWEN MYERS
owen@dazedgroup.com

digital news editor
ZING TSJENG
zing@dazedgroup.com

digital news writer
THOMAS GORTON
thomas@dazedgroup.com

production editor
ALEX DENNEY
alex.d@dazedgroup.com

social media manager
FIONA COOK
fiona.c@dazedgroup.com

social media assistant
NATASHA SLEE
natasha.s@dazedgroup.com

fashion features assistant
EMMA HOPE ALLWOOD
emma.a@dazedgroup.com

digital assistant
ASHLEIGH KANE
ashleigh@dazedgroup.com

editorial assistant
DOMINIQUE SISLEY
dominique.s@dazedgroup.com

editorial interns
LAURA AROWOLO, BIJU BELINKY,
GEORGINA EVANS, LAKEISHA
GOEDLUCK, HEATHER GWYTHER,
GEORGIA LEEFE, OLIVIA MASEK,
LYDIA MORRISH, ALEX JAMES
TAYLOR, JAMIE WATERS,
DANIELLE DE WOLFE

group editorial director
JEFFERSON HACK

group creative director
RONOJOY DAM

## contributing editors

film editor
TREY TAYLOR
trey@dazedgroup.com

music editor
AIMEE CLIFF
aimee@dazedgroup.com

visual arts editor
FRANCESCA GAVIN
art@dazedgroup.com

writers at large
CARMEN GRAY, STUART HAMMOND,
HANNAH LACK, SUSANNE MADSEN
KIN WOO

## text

LEONIE COOPER , MHAIRI GRAHAM,
CLAIRE HEALY, DAISY JONES,
SUSANNE MADSEN, JAMES MERRY,
KATE NEAVE, LIZ PELLY, NATALIE
RIGG, CAROLINE RYDER, PATRIK
SANDBERG, ANTWAUN SARGENT,
MAXWELL WILLIAMS

## photography

MICHAEL AVEDON, JEFF BARK,
RICHARD BURBRIDGE, DARIO
CATELLANI, RACHEL CHANDLER,
FELIX COOPER, PIERRE
DEBUSSCHERE, JOHNNY DUFORT,
SHARIF HAMZA, GREG HARRIS,
NICK HAYMES, JEFF HENRIKSON,
DREW JARRETT, JAI ODELL, SEAN
AND SENG, CASPER SEJERSEN

## thanks to
ROY and ANNE WADDELL
ALEX BETTS

REPROGRAPHICS BY TAPESTRY
PRINTED BY WYNDEHAM ROCHE

## fashion

fashion director
ROBBIE SPENCER
robbie@dazedgroup.com

fashion editors
ELIZABETH FRASER-BELL
elizabeth@dazedgroup.com

EMMA WYMAN
emma@dazedgroup.com

beauty editor
YADIM

senior contributing
fashion editors
HANNES HETTA
TONY IRVINE
JACOB K
MATTIAS KARLSSON
KAREN LANGLEY
KATIE SHILLINGFORD

contributing fashion
editors
AGATA BELCEN
JOHN COLVER
CELESTINE COONEY
ELLIE GRACE CUMMING
TOM GUINNESS
NELL KALONJI
ADAM WINDER

executive fashion editors
CATHY EDWARDS
KATY ENGLAND
NICOLA FORMICHETTI
ALISTER MACKIE

fashion assistants
LIZY CURTIS
lizy@dazedgroup.com

SAMIA GIOBELLINA
samia@dazedgroup.com

fashion interns
ABI FASHESIN, ANNA KNOTT,
KATHARINA STARK

casting director
NOAH SHELLEY

RANKIN PHOTOGRAPHY
020 7284 7320
info@rankin.co.uk

©2014 DAZED
Published by Waddell Limited
Registered address:
112 –116 Old Street,
London EC1V 9BG
tel 020 7336 0766
fax 020 7336 0966

SUBMISSIONS
dazed@dazedgroup.com

dazeddigital.com
twitter.com/dazedmagazine
facebook.com/
dazedandconfusedmagazine

SUBSCRIPTIONS
For all subscriptions go to
dazeddigital.com

One year's print subscription (six
issues) with free digital subscription:
UK £20
Europe £25
Americas $38
Rest of the world £40

Digital subscription only:
£15 per year

The digital subscription consists of
an online version of the magazine,
with free access to 20 years of
Dazed archives alongside Apple App
and Android versions.

From the UK, Europe and the rest of
the world, post to:
Dazed c/o CMS, Unit 25–26
Bermondsey Trading Estate, Rother-
hithe, New Road, London, SE16 3LL
0203 751 4406
subs@cmsnetwork.co.uk

All credit / debit card payments
will be debited in the name of
Waddell Limited.

## design

creative director
CHRISTOPHER SIMMONDS

digital art director
JENNY CAMPBELL-COLQUHOUN
jenny@dazedgroup.com

designers
HANNAH FINCHAM
hannah.m.f@dazedgroup.com

JUSTIN DEVON MOORE
justin@dazedgroup.com

design intern
HALIMA OLALEMI

## photography

acting photographic editor
SAORLA HOUSTON
saorla@dazedgroup.com

photographic assistant
AARO MURPHY
aaro@dazedgroup.com

photographic intern
STEPHANIE WILSON

## digital design and production

digital development
manager
MATT JONES
mattj@dazedgroup.com

technical lead
LUKE SPICE
luke@dazedgroup.com

web developer
PHILIP RATCLIFFE
philip@dazedgroup.com

front end web developer
DANIEL ADEYEMI
dan@dazedgroup.com

## production

group production manager
GENEVIEVE WAITES
eve@dazedgroup.com

print and reprographics manager
STEVE SAVIGEAR
steve@dazedgroup.com

## video

acting head of video
JENNIFER BYRNE
jennifer@dazedgroup.com

junior production manager
CAMILLA MATHIS
camilla@dazedgroup.com

development assistant
KATE VILLEVOYE
kate@dazedgroup.com

post-production assistant
ALEX TOWNLEY
alex.t@dazedgroup.com

video interns
NATALIE FAIRS, RYAN ONEILL

## advertising & creative solutions

group ad director
PRIYA DE SOUZA
priya@dazedgroup.com
020 7549 6867

senior account managers
HEATHER JEMETTA
heather@dazedgroup.com
020 7549 6822

LYDIA DEWDNEY-PALA
lydia@dazedgroup.com
020 7549 6878

account manager
TOMMY SERES
tommy@dazedgroup.com

advertising account executive
ALEX BROWN
alex@dazedgroup.com
020 7549 6847

digital ad account executive
TAMSIN WEIR
tamsin@dazedgroup.com

creative projects manager
ABIGAIL SUTTON
abi.s@dazedgroup.com
020 7549 6833

creative projects coordinator
ANNIE HALL
annie@dazedgroup.com

digital ad trafficker
CHRISTOPHER SABIN
christopher@dazedgroup.com
020 7549 6833

advertising interns
TANIA KABBANI
MADELEINE ROBERTS

foreign advertising agents
ITALY - JB MEDIA
+39 02 29013427

JEFFREY BYRNES
jeffrey@jbmedia.com

GEORGIA GAY
georgia@jbmedia.com

account
JILL BYRNES
jill@jbmedia.com

editorial and pr director
FRANCESCA FREGOSI
fra@jbmedia.com

## white label

global partnership director
NICOLE ELIAS
nicole@dazedgroup.com

creative strategist
JONNY KANAGASOORIAM
jonny@dazedgroup.com

account manager
DOMINIQUE FENN
dominique@dazedgroup.com

project manager
FELICITY SHAW
felicity@dazedgroup.com

## marketing, events and pr

marketing director
EMMA SUTTON
emma.s@dazedgroup.com

events manager
LUCY WARWICK
lucy@dazedgroup.com

pr and branding manager
HANNAH MOTH
hannah.moth@dazedgroup.com

marketing and events assistant
ALISHA CROMPTON
alisha@dazedgroup.com

digital marketing coordinator
SEAN CARPENTER
sean@dazedgroup.com

Marketing interns
MARC MACDONALD

us pr and marketing consultant
MANDIE ERIKSEN,
SEVENTH HOUSE PR
mandie@showroomseven.com
+1 212 643 4810

## publishing

publishers
RANKIN WADDELL
JEFFERSON HACK

associate publisher
ROB MONTGOMERY
rob@dazedgroup.com

publishing director
SUSANNE WADDELL
susanne@dazedgroup.com

publishing manager
LIAM KELLY
liam@dazedgroup.com

rankin's manager
SANDRA BARRON

pa to group editorial director
OLGA KENNY
olga@dazedgroup.com

it and systems manager
JAMES BAKER
james.b@dazedgroup.com

hr manager
SARAH LYNCH
sarah@dazedgroup.com

office coordinator
FINN ATKINS
finn@dazedgroup.com

front of house
CLAUDIA ROSE SHAW
claudia.s@dazedgroup.com

## distribution

circulation manager
STUART WHITE
stuart@dazedgroup.com
+44 207 549 6813

worldwide distribution
COMAG
01895 433 800

subscription enquiries
dazed@ocsmedia.net
+44 207 640 3898

syndication manager
TATSUO HINO
syndication@dazedgroup.com

## international editions

DAZED & CONFUSED KOREA
is published by MEDIA BLING

ceo & publisher
SEHOON LEE
sehoon@dazeddigital.co.kr

editor-in-chief
YOONJUNG YANG
yjyang@dazeddigital.co.kr

syndication
SANGHEE LEE
sanghew@dazeddigital.co.kr
tel +82 2 794 4921
fax +82 2 794 4928

info@dazeddigital.co.kr
dazeddigital.co.kr
twitter.com/dazedkorea
facebook.com/dazedkorea

## finance

financial controller
ABI BURNTON
abi@dazedgroup.com

management accountant
SADIA SALAM
sadia@dazedgroup.com

credit controller
GRETA PISTACECI
greta@dazedgroup.com

purchase ledger
NICOLE GUGA
nicole@dazedgroup.com

sales and purchase ledgers
USHA PANCHAL
usha@dazedgroup.com

MARGARET
HOWELL

DONDUP

# Spring 2015

This issue is about extreme personalities. We toast the cultural anarchists who have changed the world by never compromising their artistic vision. People like Rei Kawakubo, Björk, Marilyn Manson, Jean Paul Gaultier, Alexander McQueen, Gregg Araki, Genesis Breyer P-Orridge, and Harmony Korine – each of whom you're about to see in a whole new light.

Cover star Yo-landi Visser is in many ways the torchbearer for today's culture of extremes. She gives zero fucks about what people think about her and it's paying off. As part of zef-rap rave crew Die Antwoord, she and Ninja have created a viral music revolution through the sheer force of their personalities. Few could have predicted their meteoric rise, let alone myself.

I first met the group back in 2010 at a Wimpy restaurant in Cape Town. They had been famous for exactly 56 days, after their video for "Enter the Ninja" had unexpectedly blown up. We spent the day and night driving around the city and Cape Flats, hanging out in squats and government housing projects with rats and eating pizza with gangsta rappers. They were about to fly to the US to sign a deal with Interscope and play Coachella. Their lives were set to change forever, but no-one knew how long Die Antwoord could ride the buzz wave for.

Fast-forward five years, and the wave has turned into a tsunami. Cara Delevingne now pops up in their videos and Aphex Twin sends them beats to rap over. They have more than 200 million views on their YouTube channels, and are about to star alongside Sigourney Weaver in Neill Blomkamp's sci-fi blockbuster *Chappie*. It's insane what they've achieved.

So we thought it would be cool to look at life through Yo-landi Visser's onyx eyes. In her first major solo interview, she tells Caroline Ryder about her struggles as a young mum, the power of *that* peroxide mullet, and how she turned down a starring role in David Fincher's *The Girl with the Dragon Tattoo*.

Elsewhere, Trey Taylor meets Amalia Ulman, the Insta-celebrity who became infamous for faking a boob job in the name of art; Björk and philosopher Oddný Eir discuss desire and heartbreak; and trans rocker Laura Jane Grace talks self-identity. Oh yeah, Marilyn Manson also calls me a cunt and threatens to put a gun in my mouth. Is that extreme enough for you?

Tim Noakes
Editor-in-Chief
@DazedMagazine

CAROLINE RYDER
The LA-based writer met with cover star and "matriarchal leader of the super-freak elite" Yo-landi Visser to talk motherhood and Hollywood (p. 154). "I was expecting attitude but got none. She was polite, present, intuitive and honest," recalls Ryder. "One of the realest interview subjects ever." After moving to the Mojave desert in 2010, Ryder is now finishing her MFA in screenwriting under the tutelage of *Mulholland Drive*'s Mary Sweeney.

*What would be your zef-rap alter-ego?*
Mi$$y Von Raptop.

*What three celeb cameos would you have in your rap video?*
Miranda July, Kurt Vile's brother who makes jello-shots, and that cool pope who's in the Vatican right now.

*What would be the title of your reality show?*
The Real Perpetually Underwhelmed Housewives of Hollywood.

EMMA WYMAN
Dazed's fashion editor turned shopping bags into headwear for model Lexi Boling in Splitting Image, her story shot by Sean and Seng (p. 216). She also flew out to LA for our Marilyn Manson feature (p. 182) and Hollywood's Anti-Heroines (p. 116).

*What was it like styling Marilyn?*
Surreal. He told me all the 'Manson girls' would kill me for putting him in latex and a corset. Although he did keep the corset for his tour.

*What's the most extreme item in your closet?*
A Helmut Lang sequinned coat with hidden bondage straps.

MOLLY BAIR
After being surrounded by blood-red roses and hunks of rotting meat for our Comme des Garçons shoot (p. 166), you'd think model-of-the-moment Molly would fancy a lie-down. "It was just a typical day on the job," the 17-year-old shrugs, with the same IDGAF attitude she brought to the SS15 runways of Chanel, Prada and Dior.

*What's your beautiful dark twisted fantasy?*
Eating grapes and cheese on a Greek island with Kanye West.

*Freddy Krueger or Jason Voorhees?*
Freddy, for sure. He's everything you'd want in a villain: lack of skincare, bad style, unphotogenic.

*If you were in a gory movie, how would you like to die?*
Me? Dying? No! I'm far too selfish for that to happen.

NATALIE RIGG
In anticipation of McQueen's sell-out Savage Beauty show at the V&A, London-based fashion writer Natalie Rigg immersed herself in the magical and macabre world of the legendary designer (p. 110).

*Armadillo heels or butterfly hat?*
Armadillo heels – grotesque and beautiful at once.

*High-rise or bumster?*
Bumster. They're a bit crude, but there's something really elegant about the way they elongate the upper body.

*Who would you most like to give an extreme makeover?*
Kate Middleton (for obvious reasons).

FENDI

JEFF HENRIKSON
Shot Marilyn Manson,
page 182 and
"Hollywood's Anti-
Heroines", page 116

*What was the weirdest
thing that you
encountered in Marilyn
Manson's house?*
There were a lot of
interesting things.
I would have to say
the most memorable was
a portrait of Elvis
painted by John
Wayne Gacy (known as
the Killer Clown).

*What would you make
illegal if you could?*
Groups of people
loitering in the
middle of sidewalks.

*If your life was made
into a film, what
would the genre be?*
Comedy, because I
hate drama.

*Who would play you
in the movie of
your life?*
Jerry Seinfeld.

MICHAEL AVEDON
Shot Gregg Araki, page 126

*What's the most extreme situation
you've found yourself in?*
When I was caught on the inside of
the reef while surfing Lances Right
in the Mentawai Islands, Indonesia.
Also when I was surfing overhead
waves at Soup Bowl in Barbados –
quite a heavy wave indeed.

*If you could make one thing illegal,
what would it be?*
Guns – they have proven to be the
downfall of humanity.

# Snapshots
### Near-death wipeouts, serial-killer portraits and a bevy of belfies – this issue's photographers get in the mood for some extreme behaviour

PIERRE DEBUSSCHERE
Shot Yo-landi Visser,
page 154

*What was it like shooting
Yo-landi for our cover?*
Intense.

*What would be your zef-rap
alter-ego?*
'Moumoule'.

*Which extreme icon would you
most like to photograph?*
Björk – I've looked up to
her since I was a kid.

*What would you make illegal
if you could?*
Heartbreak.

*What song makes you
completely lose yourself?*
'Stay out Here' by
The Knife.

**DARIO CATELLANI**
Shot Amalia Ulman,
page 192

*Would you ever fake
a luxury lifestyle
for Instagram likes?*
Nah, I wouldn't.
But I do find
douchey Instagrams
quite entertaining.

*What is one
Instagram brag you
are totally over?*
The ones that
hashtag things
like #gang, #love,
#family and #fun.

*Who's your Instagram
guilty pleasure
and why?*
My wife. Damn,
she's so much more
interesting than
I am!

*Selfies or belfies?*
Belfies, for sure.
Needed to Google
'belfies', though.

**SHARIF HAMZA**
Shot "Caught in the Act",
page 256

*What's the most drastic
decision you've ever made?*
Moving to New York.

*What song makes you completely
lose yourself?*
'Purple Rain' by Prince.

*What would you make illegal if
you could?*
Reality TV shows running for
more than one season.

*What situation makes you the
most anxious?*
Hearing about people's
addiction to reality TV.

**SEAN AND SENG**
Shot "Splitting
Image", page 216

*Who do you prefer to
shoot - the good girl
or the bad girl?*
The girl that's very
bad at being good.

*If you were sent to
hell, who would you
take with you?*
If one of us is going,
we're both going.

*Who's your favourite
villain of all time?*
The Big Bad Wolf.
Gotta love a wolf
that dresses up as
a grandma.

*How did you get the
fly to stay on Lexi
Boling's face?*
Lexi is our Venus
flytrap.

Iceberg
Downtown Gallery

40 years of creative
dialogues

1974

Sandy Kim, photographer
New York City

photo Olivier Zahm

2015

# ICEBERG

# Turn to the dark side

**Experimental milliner Noel Stewart tips his hat to J.W.Anderson**

"If a woman has a penchant for warm leatherette, then she'll be wearing this to the beach. There's nowhere better to throw some shade than *sur la plage*. An image of a giant, sheer sun hat was the starting point when working with J.W.Anderson on this, but obviously we took it in a different direction. Just remember, a floppy hat is no substitute for sunscreen – we're making fashion here, not curing cancer!"

Text Trey Taylor  Photography Felix Cooper  Styling Adam Winder
all clothes and accessories by J.W.Anderson

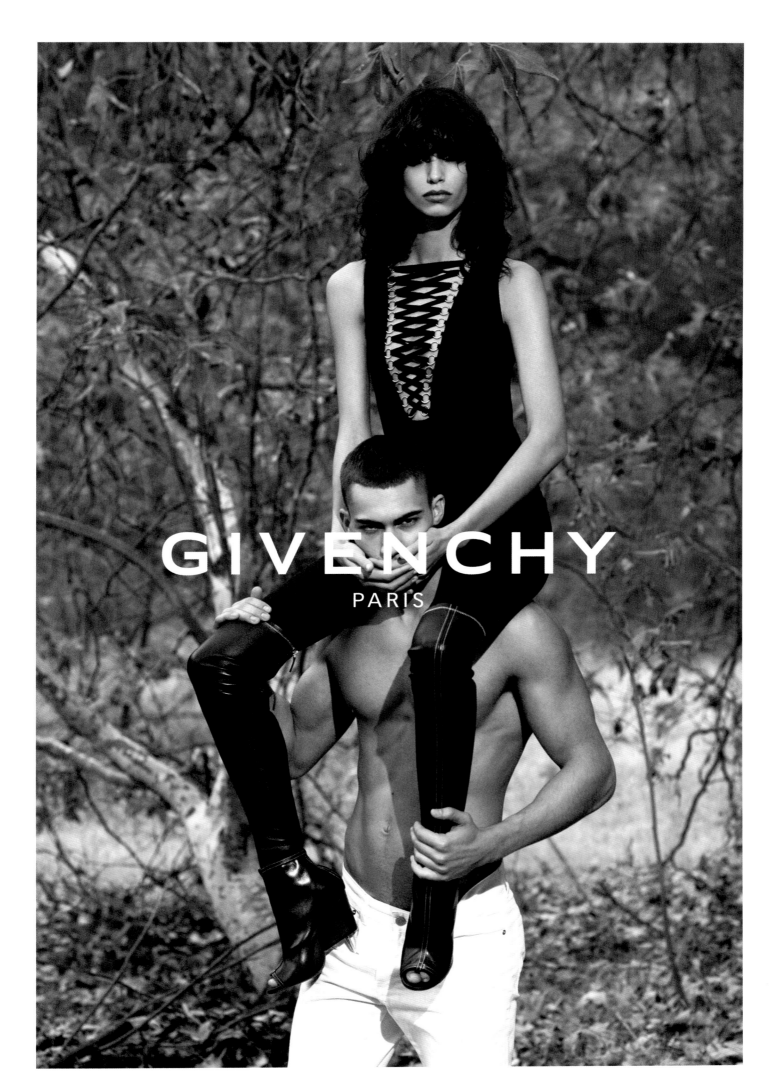

# Riff it up

**Belly-baring singer Kali Uchis cuts it short with MBMJ's crop top**

"When I wear a midriff top, I feel like 'Candy' by Cameo should start playing. I'd pair this print with a fruity cocktail that has an umbrella in. The items I'd stick into my crop top for a fun night out? A bow tie in case things need to get professional, and an inhaler in case things get too out of control."

all clothes by Marc by Marc Jacobs

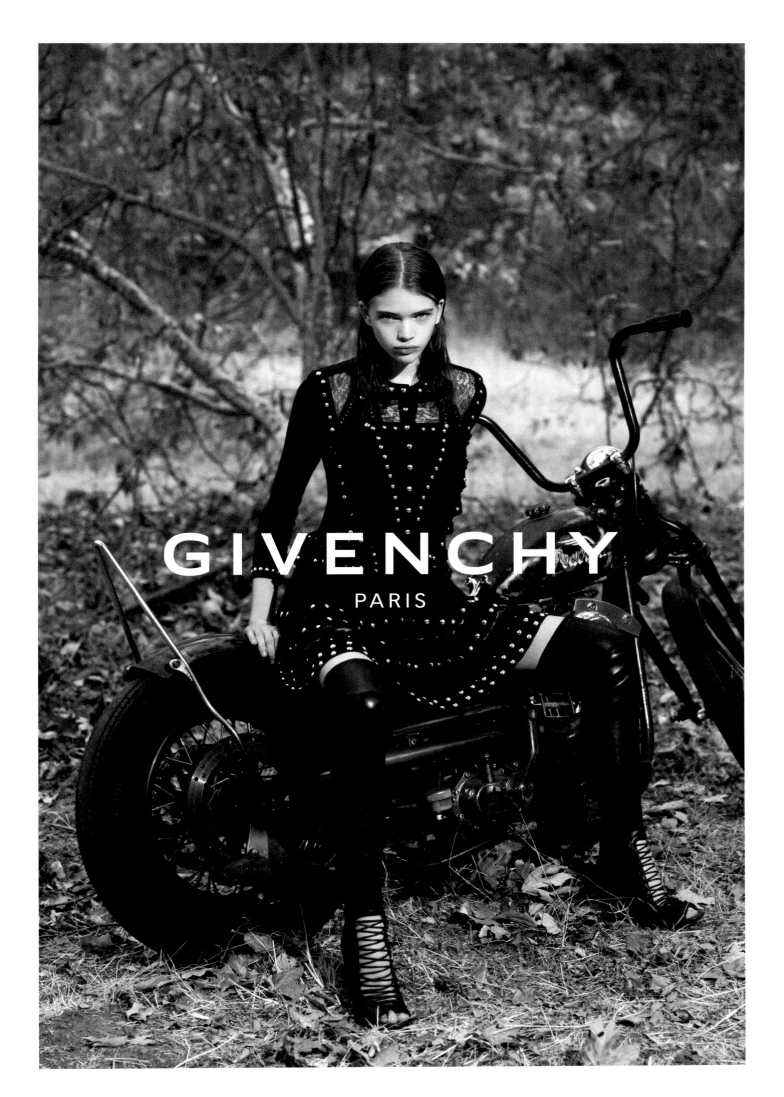

GIVENCHY

PARIS

# Snap out of it

**Raf Simons summons the spirit of youth with his nostalgic patched jacket**

"It's about memories, but it's also about things we all experience. The collection started with the love between my parents. From there it's me growing up, starting the label, meeting people... I'm representing things in a way that's challenging. Like a rollercoaster, it's exciting but it's also dangerous."

all clothes and accessories by Raf Simons

Artist Anne-Lise Coste
(MAYBE I WILL FEEL) BETTER

COMME des GARÇONS SHIRT
*

# Get in the ring

**Accessories obsessive Mademoiselle Yulia spaces out with Louis Vuitton**

"Are they sci-fi-inspired? They would be perfect for Barbarella! Personally, I would team these with my orange dress, wavy hair and a red ribbon on my head. Or there's a vintage Barbie from the late 60s called 'Twist 'N Turn' which would suit these earrings perfectly. I can be larger than life, but earrings can never be too big."

all clothes and accessories by Louis Vuitton

# MOSCHINO

# Tie to the thigh

**Givenchy muse
Jamie Bochert gets
knee-deep in
Riccardo Tisci's boots**

"Should you mix womenswear and menswear? Of course! I would love to see these on a naked male stripper. Even though they're from the men's line, I would pair them with my long black archive Givenchy gown. Riccardo's vision is authentic – when I look at his work, I see art, music and life. It's everything."

all clothes and accessories by Givenchy by Riccardo Tisci

# M·A·C
# LONDON
**AUTUMN/WINTER 2015**
**MACCOSMETICS.TUMBLR.COM**

# the secret history of Alexander McQueen

Whether stacking models on a heap of rotten food or challenging body stereotypes in his groundbreaking, guest-edited Fashion-Able issue, Dazed's iconic fashion editor-at-large Alexander McQueen used the magazine to rewrite fashion's rulebook. To celebrate landmark retrospective Savage Beauty coming to the V&A, the designer's collaborators recall his most extreme moments from our archive.

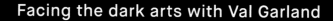

## Facing the dark arts with Val Garland

"This collection was an exploration of the sinister side of childhood, and Lee (McQueen) took his inspiration from the 80s US slasher film *Child's Play*. We created this extreme beauty look that turned runway models into macabre clowns. Nobody but Lee would have dared to do this. I felt like we were part of history in the making. We needed girls with simple features and strong bone structure that could be used as a blank canvas. Acrylic make-up wasn't available back then, so I used thick theatre paints and blanked out the face, then drew black graphic patterns around the eyes, nose and mouth. I remember Lee examining the models and saying, 'Let's push it further!' He never wanted to play it safe. There was an enormous amount of energy backstage at the show that day, as there always was when Lee was around. We all wanted to go that extra mile for him. The stark, shadowy lighting made the hair and make-up seem so much more intense. I think that's caught on camera here – these images really capture the darkness of McQueen."

Text Natalie Rigg
Image issue 78 (June 2001) Alexander McQueen AW01/02 Photography Martina Hoogland Ivanow Styling Katy England Hair Guido Make-up Val Garland

IMMACULATE

REPLAY

## Smashing watermelons with Norbert Schoerner

"The story was never a literal interpretation of (Pier Paolo Pasolini's notorious last film) *Salò*, though it explored some of the plot's touchstones, such as sex and death. We shot it in this enormous derelict factory in east London. There were no storyboards, just a loose concept – Lee would always encourage that freedom to create and was happy to go where the process took him. I feel this is the most powerful image from the story. We approached it as a still-life because of the naturalistic quality of all the food. It has a biblical dimension and a sort of medieval texture. The placid expressions on the models' faces became especially memorable: I think we both knew we were skirting the edges of taste. As we started draping the three of them on this huge mound of pigs' heads and rotting food to look as though they were dead, suddenly the atmosphere became very intense. It was a warm day so the smell was really pungent, too. I remember Lee running around smashing watermelons on set to add to the pile. He was always so hands-on with each composition."

Image issue 81 (September 2001)  Concept Alexander McQueen  Photography Norbert Schoerner  Hair Guido  Make-up Val Garland

DROMe

## Chasing butterflies with Katy England

"The Fashion-Able issue of Dazed spoke to Lee's belief that beauty can be found in extreme difference and individuality. Each of the real models we cast in the shoot had a different physical disability and I know it was very important to him that they felt at ease and could trust our vision, knowing that we all wanted to achieve something beautiful. He had asked some of his most respected peers, such as Hussein Chalayan, Rei Kawakubo and milliner Philip Treacy, to custom-create pieces for each subject. For Sue Bramley, who was blind, Treacy dreamed up this incredible, ornate butterfly headpiece that trailed down the forehead, protecting the eyes. Nature was a recurring theme in Lee's work and he felt that the butterflies had a romantic, elegant quality. I remember him describing the piece in great detail to her, so that she could get a sense of how it might appear. I think we all felt humbled that day. It was the most challenging project we'd ever done and certainly the most unique experience for everybody involved."

Image issue 46 (September 1998)  Concept Alexander McQueen  Photography Nick Knight  Styling Katy England  Butterfly hat by Philip Treacy  Research and production Zoe Bradley
Alexander McQueen: Savage Beauty runs at the V&A in London March 14–August 2

Shaving your hair into a mohawk and starring in an STD-themed horror isn't exactly a well-trodden path to Hollywood hype – but there's a new gang of girls ripping up Tinseltown with fireball force and a taste for the extreme

Hair Sylvia Wheeler at Atelier Management  Make-up Gloria Noto at Atelier Management  Styling assistants Virginia Fontaine, Cassie Walker  Special thanks Rich Tigpen and Miguel Chenal

hollywood's anti-heroines

## Taissa Farmiga

Grabbing a five-finger discount chez Paris Hilton in *The Bling Ring* (2013) was only a warm-up for Taissa Farmiga. After playing a teen witch in *American Horror Story*, the 20-year-old Jersey girl will star in 80s-set horror flick *The Final Girls* this year. "Let's just say we had to deal with some extremes," she laughs. "Running in the blazing sun and screaming until we nearly passed out – and then sprinting through a forest, soaked and shivering."

Text Trey Taylor  Photography Jeff Henrikson  Styling Emma Wyman
Taissa wears leather shirt by DROMe; paillette skirt by Burberry Prorsum; snakeskin shoes by Salvatore Ferragamo

## Odeya Rush

Starring in Coach's AW14 campaign is just a footnote in Odeya Rush's whirlwind career – she fronted sci-fi flick *The Giver* last year, and will return in a *Léon*-esque thriller, *Hunter's Prayer*, in 2015. "While filming I learned how to shoot a gun, take it apart and put it back together," the 17-year-old says. "And I can do it fast." Come next spring, she'll be reviving a generation's childhood nightmares alongside Jack Black in *Goosebumps*.

Odeya wears leather and wool blazer by The Koopies; denim dress (worn underneath) by AllSaints; printed cotton shirt by Jil Sander Navy

## Joey King

Putting the buzz in 'buzz cut', Joey King has shaved her head twice for roles in *The Dark Knight Rises* (2012) and *Wish I Was Here* (2014). The 15-year-old actress also stars in longtime mentor James Franco's Faulkner adaptation *The Sound and the Fury*, which she says "brought out my inner Beyoncé – with a dash of a 1920s southern accent." Up next? "I'm producing a movie. We start filming this month."

Joey wears wool and chiffon knitted jumper by Avant Toi; diamond earring worn in right ear Joey's own; safety pin earring worn in left ear stylist's own

# #EVERYDAYLIFE
*Stockholm*

## Rosa Salazar

"I can be just as hard as Lynn in *Insurgent*," says Rosa Salazar of her role in the *Divergent* series' latest instalment (out March 20), for which she chose to sport an "intense" mohawk haircut. "We've both faced adversity. I am equally pissed off." The 23-year-old Marylander has clearly acquired a taste for the high-octane – this autumn, she'll take a lead role in telepathic teen sci-fi *The Maze Runner: Scorch Trials*.

Rosa wears silk jumpsuit by Dondup

Sebastian Sauve for Les Benjamins, Spring Summer 2015
lesbenjamins.com

LES BENJAMINS

## Maika Monroe

In cult classic-to-be *It Follows* (out Feb 27), Maika Monroe's character loses her virginity and her mind, as she's hounded by the feeling that she is being stalked. "Just a normal girl who is met with a harrowing paranormal situation," the 21-year-old Cali native deadpans of the STD-allegory horror. After starring in a slew of indies, she'll come out guns blazing opposite Chloë Grace Moretz in alien invasion thriller *The Fifth Wave*, due in January 2016.

Maika wears faux-fur coat by Coach; sequinned dress by Jil Sander Navy; silk shirt (worn underneath) by AllSaints; suede lace-up sandals by Chloé

**www.carhartt-wip.com**

Photography by Joshua Gordon, artwork by Tim Head

**carhartt**®
WORK IN PROGRESS

## Ana Lily Amirpour

"The most shocking thing is that a black-and-white Iranian vampire film made it into American movie theatres," says director Ana Lily Amirpour of *A Girl Walks Home Alone at Night*. Out later this year, her first film chronicles a lonely female vampire stalking the streets of a ghost town. So after revamping the bloodsucker genre, what will she do next? "A dystopian cannibal love story set in a Texan wasteland called *The Bad Batch*."

Ana Lily wears jersey t-shirt by Replay; silk trousers by Ilaria Nistri

ALEXA ★ CHUNG FOR AG

SPRING 2015

# Gregg Araki

## apocalypse now and again

Gregg Araki is the maestro of modern desperation and teen rage. With films such as *The Living End*, *Mysterious Skin* and *The Doom Generation*, the indie director unleashed an incandescent, post-new wave aesthetic that informed an entire generation and looks equally at home on the Cannes Croisette as it does in your cult classic Netflix queue. With new movie *White Bird in a Blizzard*, a murder mystery in which Shailene Woodley gets her sexual awakening on screen, he revisits the 1980s, the era that made him as an artist, and comes to his most disturbing conclusion yet: somewhere along the way to total annihilation, Gregg Araki grew up.

Text Patrik Sandberg  Photography Michael Avedon  Styling Natasha Newman-Thomas
Gregg wears suit by BOSS; cotton shirt by Dior Homme

*Boredom and looming apocalypse are themes which have recurred in your work since your first film,* Three Bewildered People in the Night *(1987). Where do you stand on these ideas now?*
We live in very weird, apocalyptic times. *Three Bewildered People* was 28 years ago. The world that we live in now feels very much like *The Doom Generation* (1995), with global warming... The Sony hacking thing really freaked me out. It feels a bit like the beginning of the end. But then there's the idea that it has always kind of felt that way. There was Y2K, the atom bomb, the Aids crisis... My first movies were very much a diary for me. They were very personal; it was almost like therapy. *White Bird* is looking back at those feelings from the perspective of somebody who is older and hopefully wiser.

*Something that ties the protagonists of your films together is their sense of hopelessness. Why are you drawn to these characters?*
For me it's always been about the outsiders; the people who aren't in the mainstream. Maybe it's the generation I'm from. I just grew up at the exact right moment: I was in high school when the Sex Pistols came out, and all through college, when I was finding myself and the period in which *White Bird* is set, was the explosion of post-punk and alternative music. It was all about being different; having your own voice and your own ideas. And it was a big influence on me – it really is what formulated my sensibility.

*And then there's the homosexuality...*
That's another thing. I grew up in this open, exciting period with new wave music and crazy artistic expression and performance art and goth clubs. It was important for me to grow up in that atmosphere, but there was also the bonus of being gay or queer in that world – I was always the outsider, always different, always approaching things from a different point of view. As an artist, that's a huge advantage.

*You won the first Queer Palm at Cannes, and you are often pegged as a 'gay director', even though your films feature characters of every sexual orientation. Do you think Hollywood has faced the reality of homosexuality in the last 20 years?*
I think it has, in a lot of ways. The world has changed a lot since *The Living End* (1992) came out. That film was so shocking and radical at the time in terms of its portrayal of gay desire. You look back on it now and it all seems so quaint. I don't watch *How to Get Away With Murder* but I've heard about it, and the fact that they have these pretty steamy gay sex scenes on primetime television, that was unheard of in the early 90s. But back then nobody would have imagined gay people would be getting married in the US. So things have changed, which is obviously great. But it's just like racism. Things have changed, but they also haven't changed. There's still ignorance. But there has been a remarkable step forward, I think.

*Would you ever direct a Hollywood blockbuster?*
I've got nothing against doing a studio movie. I would love to do a *Twin Peaks*-type TV show and direct a pilot. But it would have to be something I'm passionate about. The bigger the movie or show, the more it has to make economic sense. You can't make something niche like *The Doom Generation* on a huge budget, it's just not very responsible.

I have a script now that's a genre project that's very commercial. It's still very much one of my movies, but it has elements that are very marketable so it can support a larger budget.

*I heard you were currently working on a new project,* The Womb?
That's one of them! I work on a few projects at the same time, so hopefully it'll happen sooner rather than later. It's a script that was given to me years ago and I did a rewrite on it. It's sort of like *Seven* or *Zodiac*, it's this really dark serial-killer type of thriller, but it has a lot of thematic things that are very in line with my other movies. It makes sense. It's not like, 'Oh, direct *Step Up 4*.' (*laughs*) But they're past *Step Up 4* now, aren't they?

*I'm not sure! I think it's a 3D thing now.*
Hey, they gave the world Channing Tatum! For better or for worse, we have Channing Tatum because of *Step Up*.

*You made* Totally Fucked Up *(1993) on very little budget without permits, yet it's one of your most beautiful films. What is the biggest budget you've had to work with?*
The biggest budget in the range of *Splendor* (1999) was $3 million I think, and *Smiley Face* (2007) was also in the $2 million range. All of them are tiny movies even by indie standards. Look at 'indie' movies like *The Grand Budapest Hotel*. That movie probably cost $20 million. It's a completely different ballpark. But it's true, the early movies like *The Living End* and *Totally Fucked Up* were made for about $20,000, which is nothing. *Totally Fucked Up* was made, of all things, with an NEA (National Endowment for the Arts) grant. It's so much easier to do that now than it was in the early 90s. We didn't have things like Final Cut and all the things that kids today have.

*What does* White Bird in a Blizzard *say about who you are today?*
It's more serious, it's more classical. In a weird way, it's not just a coming-of-age story, it's also a coming of age (for me personally). It has thematic consistencies with my other movies, but it's also tackling different things – I was able to stretch myself. The last scene with Eva Green and Chris Meloni is the best scene I've directed in my life. When I saw it come together for the first time I was kind of blown away. I remember in *Mysterious Skin* (2004) when we shot that scene where the kids are in the car and that redneck guy pulls a gun – that scene to me was so much fun to shoot, but I can do that in my sleep.

*You've done your own versions of the road movie, the arthouse film, the crime caper, the teen flick and more besides. Now, with* White Bird in a Blizzard, *you're doing the murder mystery. Was it your intention to reinvent these tropes?*
I didn't want to make *The Living End* or *The Doom Generation* again. But there are certain contemporary filmmakers – I won't name them – that do the same fucking movie over and over and it's really boring. You change as you get older. Every movie I've made is different, but it's because *I'm* different. I'm not the same person I was in 1992 or 1999.

White Bird in a Blizzard is out on March 6

# Collective Evolution
## the crystal visions of swarovski

Rodarte SS15

From the jewelled bird's nest hats of Alexander McQueen to Hussein Chalayan's futuristic bubble dress, Swarovski has been instrumental in creating some of the most iconic pieces of the past 15 years. But how did an Austrian jewellery empire end up nurturing a generation of designers? It began with a friendship struck up between Nadja Swarovski and late fashion editor Isabella Blow, which led to a collaboration with McQueen for SS99. The collection laid the foundations for the Swarovski Collective, a programme offering year-long financial support to emerging designers and use of the brand's coveted crystals in their designs. Now Swarovski and Dazed are teaming up this spring to host an exhibition marking 15 years of the initiative, which has championed some of this century's boldest talents including Iris van Herpen and Rodarte, and remains at the vanguard of the industry today. "Swarovski is so far removed from the grungy, dishevelled look we love and work on," say Marques'Almeida of their glittering SS15 show with the collective. "So it was incredible to create something by putting these two very different attitudes together."

Text Mhairi Graham  Photography Jai Odell  Styling Nell Kalonji
details of the Swarovski Collective exhibition will be announced via Dazed Digital

Viktor & Rolf SS09

Ashley Williams SS15

Iris van Herpen SS15

Hussein Chalayan SS07

Marques'Almeida SS15

# Meredith Graves

As the singer of burning Syracuse hardcore band Perfect Pussy, Meredith Graves has spent the past year travelling the globe delivering unparalleled performances themed around trauma, control and love. The jarring aggression of her band gripped the music world, but what has resonated most strongly is Graves' own critical voice. She's articulated her feminist values through pieces for *Pitchfork* and *Rookie*, and is working on a solo record, photobook and her own label, Honor Press. "I will do literally anything I can get my hands on," she laughs. It's only as we're hearing it everywhere that you realise how badly pop culture needed her voice.

Text Liz Pelly  Photography Jai Odell  Stylist Victor Cordero
Meredith wears cotton top by The Kooples

*You made a Twitter account last year. Why?*
Because I found out that there were a lot of male music writers using Twitter to smear me and make all of these nasty comments about me. And when non-male writers come together and talk about it, we are laughing our asses off, like, 'Who is this slug-dick, receding-hairline hack motherfucker who wishes he could get close enough to smell me?' I've been thinking about the party I'm going to throw after I take down the first one who wronged me by the feet. There's going to be a piñata full of tampons and drugs. And champagne.

*You also interact with kids at shows and on Tumblr a lot.*
For some reason, people are always really surprised that I'm nice. And I have to wonder, out of the bands that we play with, who are the assholes? Who would they not approach? Because those people need help. Fuck those people.

*What have your own experiences of meeting and touring with other bands been like?*
A lot of people in popular bands are secretly shitty. It's a scary, scary world and you can make money from being a fake. If you're a woman in music, your authenticity is constantly being questioned. But when you're a guy, people take you at face value. I wish that I could talk to every teenager who is a fan of independent music in the year 2015 and say, 'I know you like these bands, but these people are not good role models.' Once I know that a person in a band is a piece of shit, I can't listen to that band any more, and I don't want to.

*It's so important that there are currently a lot of feminists and punks being given bigger platforms to project from.*
I don't want teenagers to start giving their money or their time or their energy to shitty men any earlier than they absolutely have to. I want them to have heroes who are fighters, who are survivors, who come from a diverse array of backgrounds, to give them a greater sense of how the world's systems actually operate. And more importantly, how they intersect.

*What themes from your work in Perfect Pussy do you hope will be continued through your writing and new label?*
That people who have been hurt or marginalised deserve to be heard. I have been in many countries where young kids have come up and said they were inspired by me because I came forward as someone who survived abuse and has suffered from mental illness. I have lived through a horribly abusive relationship. I have struggled my entire life with extreme depression and mood disorders. And now, after a year of travelling the world and talking to people about it, I'm in a place where I can facilitate the survival of others. Survival is an option, and once you can get to the point where you are above water, if and when you're feeling up for it, you can reach your hand back and pull someone else up.

*That's awesome.*
And even when we've had some moderate mainstream success, we're still a very far-out, weird band. I think we're a good example of how the underdog or weird kid in class can win every once in a while.

I think about Audrey Hepburn in *Funny Face*, where she's this obnoxious, intellectual girl working at a bookshop and all of a sudden someone decides she should be a model and flies her to Paris. That shit can still happen.

*How did you originally get into punk and hardcore?*
My dad listened to punk when I was growing up. We listened to Hüsker Dü a lot. My dad is punker than me by far.

*What were you like in high school?*
I did not fit in and I hated everyone. My few friends were the outcast boys. I listened to Television, Blondie, The Clash, Sonic Youth... And then there were boys in my class who told me that wasn't punk and that 'we listen to hardcore'. But what they listened to was, like, Thursday and Yellowcard! This was in the early days of Napster, so I would go home and download music, and this was how I found out about a lot of classic hardcore bands. I got into it because I knew the boys in my class couldn't possibly be right about what hardcore was. The town I'm from is so small, but we used to have a Borders at the mall, and I just devoured *Maximum Rocknroll*. So my dad, the internet and *Maximum Rocknroll* saved my life.

*Who were your teenage role models?*
I was obsessed with documentarians. There was nothing I loved more than reading biographies or histories. Growing up, the art I had access to was made by men, so I always thought I wouldn't be able to do that. But if you were a historian, you weren't part of the story, so it didn't matter what you were. That's why, when I first started getting really involved in the scene, people knew me as the girl who took photos: I was constantly photographing my friends and my life, and I still am. The first book I'm putting out on my label is my own, and it's really the first time I've ever shown anyone my photos.

*Who are your current inspirations?*
Right now, I'm really digging the Romanian author Andrei Codrescu. I think he is excellent. I read a Graham Greene book recently that I loved. People aren't my inspiration so much as activities or concepts, like the writings of Roland Barthes and Alain Badiou. There's a Desi feminist writer who is also editor-in-chief of *The New Inquiry*, Ayesha Siddiqi, whose ideas are incredible. She's half the reason I made a Twitter. I learn something from her every day.

*Reflecting back on the past 12 months, what have you learned?*
The biggest thing I've learned is that I am capable of way more than I ever thought I was. In the past year I've done more than I had done in the 25 years preceding it. I have come out of some of the worst years of my life and managed to become someone I never knew I could be. I've learned that I am not bound by my past. I don't have to be sad forever. And this to me is revolutionary.

# Heidi Bryce
## let it rip

Now in its third year, Swatch's programme of artist residencies has offered more than 100 international artists the chance to live in and reflect on the city of Shanghai as it grows rhizomatically around them. One such artist is Heidi Bryce, whose work includes cut-ups of China's "misleading" English-language media. "They don't really report what's going on," she explains. "This collage offers my impression of Chinese foreign policy." For Swatch's creative director, Carlo Giordanetti, the city is a continual inspiration. "Shanghai really is a kaleidoscope," he says. "What we provide is an environment in which the artists can breathe and express themselves."

Text Kate Neave  Image Heidi Bryce, Chinese Foreign Policy, newspaper collage (2014)

# Future Brown
## inner city sound clash

Text Maxwell Williams  Photography Nick Haymes  Styling Natasha Newman-Thomas
this page left to right: Fatima Al Qadiri wears all clothes her own; Asma Maroof wears top by Diesel, jewellery Asma's own
last page left to right: Jamie Imanian-Friedman wears all clothes his own; Daniel Pineda wears jacket by Stone Island

Springing from the same loose scene that spawned *DIS Magazine* and Hood By Air, Future Brown are a supergroup like no other. Comprising audiophile innovators Fatima Al Qadiri, Jamie Imanian-Friedman (aka J-Cush), and Asma Maroof and Daniel Pineda of Nguzunguzu, the quartet not only embody a global-minded approach to genre – and the politics tangled up therein – but thrive on this creative conflict. More than four producers in their prime coming together, Future Brown is about creating a unique lens through which to see the world, and feel its rhythms.

Meeting the four-piece in Silver Lake, Los Angeles one afternoon, the band set about unravelling the mass of influences they've conjured on their debut self-titled album, out this month. In a flash, we're plunged into a discussion of the social and cultural conditions surrounding their influences. It's a bit like being at the coolest ethnomusicology conference ever. "Grime was created by a Caribbean diaspora largely in London, in the same way that rap was created by Caribbean diaspora largely in New York," says Al Qadiri, smiling beneath her

impeccable soft-serve hairdo. "With reggaeton and dancehall, it's coming from the source. I just feel like this is the only time when you can collectively call these musical forms 'urban', because they were born in city environments. They were not 'country' music, you know? And I think that's what you search for when you live in a city as a musician – this clash of civilisations. The music of the uprooted is very interesting. The music of kuduro from Lisbon, specifically, is different from the kuduro that's coming out of Angola. I think there is a lot to be said for the music of displaced populations or people with identity crises, because people feel alienated by where they are, and they're trying to recall the 'motherland', but what's coming out is completely different."

Imanian-Friedman adjusts his cap, brow furrowed. "That's not always the case. Sometimes it's a reaction to their urban setting," he says. "And the situations going on around them. Definitely with grime and rap – with something lyrical, the content was more influenced by people's surroundings than where they were from."

"Yeah, for sure," says Al Qadiri. "Especially if you're first or second generation. There's a multitude of stories; this is just one perspective. I just think the music of diaspora is interesting and very prevalent in this project." Ideas of memory, nationalism and power have informed much of Al Qadiri's work to date. She is part of an artist collective, GCC, which takes its name from an Arab economic alliance, and she explored the idea of an "imagined China" on her 2014 release *Asiatisch*. She's known Maroof and Pineda for years. Working as Nguzunguzu, the LA-based pair drew praise for their white-hot production work on M.I.A.'s *Vicki Leekx* mixtape (2010), and subsequent releases on Fade to Mind, where they think nothing of welding baile funk and 90s South African kwaito house to a potent ghettotech beat. It squared neatly with the work that Imanian-Friedman was doing as founder of Lit City Trax, the NY-based label behind releases by late footwork legend DJ Rashad, DJ Spoko and grime artist Visionist.

While Future Brown's members may live hundreds or even thousands of miles from each other depending on the day (Al Qadiri was raised in Kuwait, but is currently between apartments), they create a new kind of electricity when they come together. "All these genres on the record work because they come from the same cultural family," says Maluca, a New York-raised singer of Dominican descent who features on their song "Vernáculo". "We're taking our shit back – the look and the music. This music is the future." On the track, Maluca seductively sings in Spanish about language, and how if you don't like what she's saying, you can kiss her ass (the Spanish word for ass, *culo*, rhyming with *vernáculo*). "The hook is cheeky," says Maluca. "'Look at my ass, kiss my ass, and get in my vernacular.'"

The song's video, an artwork unto itself, was conceived by *DIS Magazine* and released at Pérez Art Museum Miami (PAMM) during Art Basel in December last year. The clip presents a faux-beauty ad that looks legit at first, but becomes subtly more ridiculous, to the point where one model grotesquely smears lipstick on her face and another slathers cream all over her backside. "(An editor at *DIS*) used to work for L'Oréal, so he knew intimately how to construct the video," says Al Qadiri. "For instance, with beauty commercials, there's this structural element called 'reason to believe', which is when they show you the bogus science." At the PAMM launch, flyboarders in Future Brown shirts did jetpack-abetted flips over the city waterfront while Kelela, Maluca, Total Freedom and Ian Isiah performed.

The band's long-time friend Kelela features with NYC singer Isiah on "Dangerzone", the smoothest R&B moment on *Future Brown*. "I'm inspired by all of the sounds present on the record," she says. "It takes a range of elements and artists and brings them into a single context, rather than 'doing' a different sound for each track and calling it an album. This is inspiring on so many levels, but mainly because it allows the group to make connections between genres of urban music that aren't usually illuminated. It dismantles ideas of who we think is allowed to make grime, reggaeton, R&B, dancehall and so on."

As such, their debut album is packed with unlikely credits that twist their productions in startling directions. From emerging stars like Kelela and Tink to established players such as Riko Dan of Roll Deep and one-time Ludacris protege Shawnna, everyone wants to be part of Future Brown's crew. On "Talkin Bandz", Shawnna displays the same potty-mouthed aggression she channelled on her 2006 solo hit "Gettin' Some Head" – but in the radically different context of a dystopian grime beat. Meanwhile, hip hop's hottest new voice Tink features on two tracks: the club banger "Wanna Party" and the trapped and tricked-out "Room 302". Go to Dazed Digital this month to watch the video for the latter track, exclusively commissioned by the Converse x Dazed Emerging Artists Award, a prize which champions the most exciting new talent in the arts.

With this taste for the unexpected, it's no surprise that Future Brown's moniker came during a mushroom trip – in this case, taken by *DIS* founder Solomon Chase in upstate New York. The four members have worked with the NYC post-millennial media collective extensively over the years, and Al Qadiri hosted an eccentric dance radio show, Global .Wav, on

the site from 2011 to 2013. Long story short, Chase was tripping; he envisioned a colour that didn't exist on planet Earth, called it 'future brown', told Al Qadiri about it, and it just kind of stuck. But the group doesn't like to dwell on the name any more than Pearl Jam wants to answer questions about cum, especially because people pathologically try to read some hidden racial innuendo into it. "One interviewer was like, 'Are you sure it's not about race? Because I'm convinced it's about race,'" says Imanian-Friedman. "And then he tried to explain to us why it's about race."

Even so, the idea of dreaming up new shades feels apt in light of Future Brown's approach to music, which gives a platform to global sounds and genres rather than blindly appropriating them. "I want to be really honest about what I like and what aesthetic choices I make," says Pineda. "I feel like the question of (musical) freedom – 'Oh, why are you free to do that?' – is a matter of taste. How does it sound? Does it sound good? I feel like you should have freedom to make the music you like." As for their next album, the group have already laid down four instrumentals, and Maroof is dreaming of a feature with ATL rap upstarts Migos. Almost certainly, it'll include a patchwork of vocalists that might seem unrelated, but end up sounding like they're cut from the same musical cloth. Therein lies the trick: Future Brown's divine missives feel alien, magical and intangible, but at the same time worldly in a way that feels inclusive. In short? Kiss their ass, or get in their vernacular.

Future Brown is out on February 23

"We're
taking our
shit back
– this
music is
the future"
Maluca

# Yang Li and Genesis Breyer P-Orridge
## annihilate the ordinary

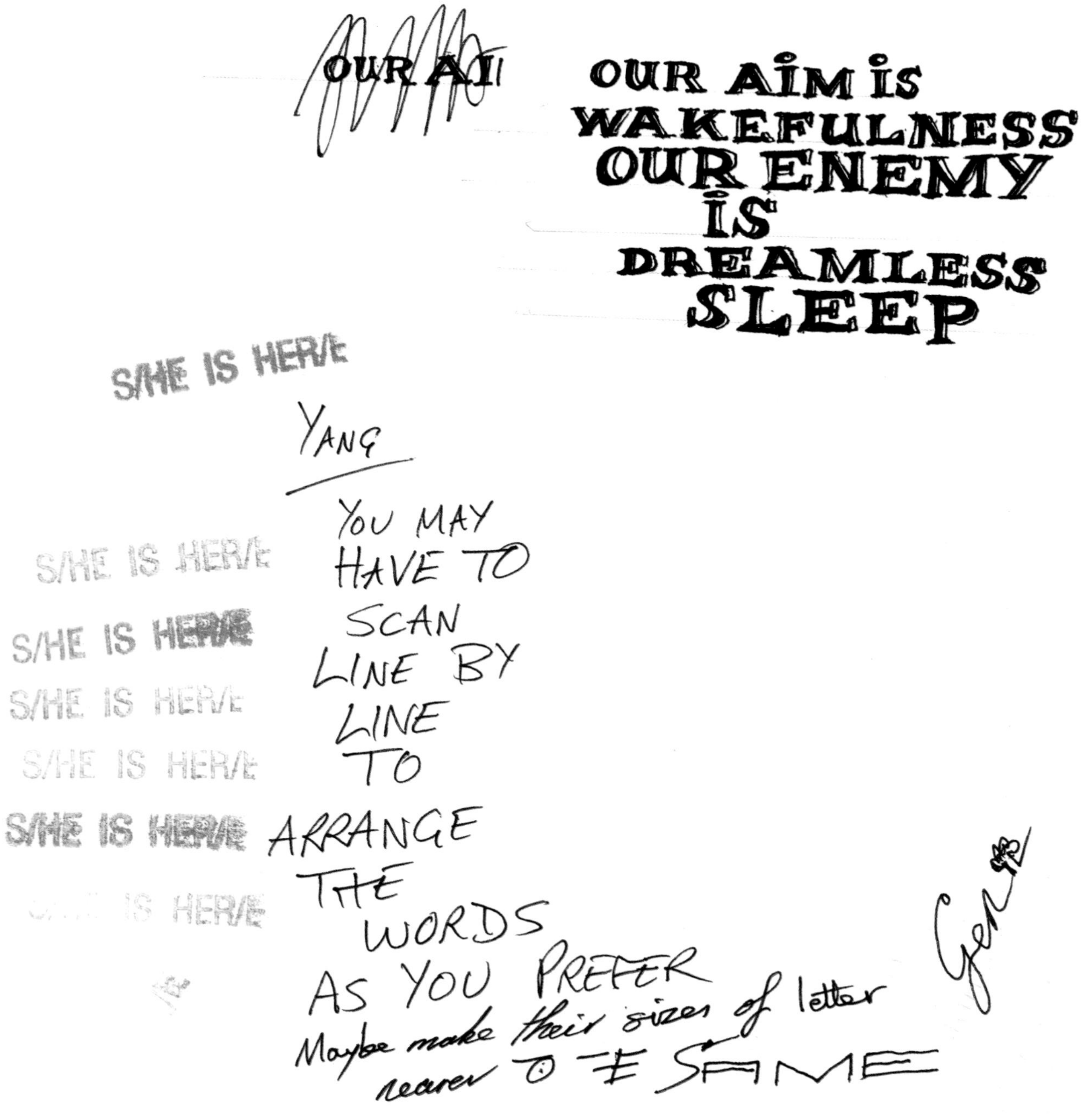

OUR AI

OUR AIM IS
WAKEFULNESS
OUR ENEMY
IS
DREAMLESS
SLEEP

S/HE IS HERE

S/HE IS HERE

S/HE IS HERE

S/HE IS HERE

S/HE IS HERE

S/HE IS HERE

S/HE IS HERE

S/HE IS HERE

YANG

YOU MAY
HAVE TO
SCAN
LINE BY
LINE
TO
ARRANGE
THE
WORDS
AS YOU PREFER
Maybe make their sizes of letter nearer O = SAME

Gen

Model Diana Set design Amy Strickland
the collaboration will launch at Selfridges as part of the AGENDER project

This season, Yang Li and Genesis Breyer P-Orridge gave us words to live by. Collaborating for the first time, the Beijing-born designer and pandrogynous icon emblazoned garments with rebellious slogans including "nothing short of a total riot, nothing short of a total war, nothing short of a total love" and "our enemy is dreamless sleep". It ignited a severe mood on the catwalk, heightened by an otherworldly soundtrack that paid tribute to paragons of the avant garde (Coil, Philip Glass and the hypnotic opening scene of Lars von Trier's 1991 film *Europa*). And if such radical concepts seem ill-suited to a sphere not regularly confronted with profound existential quandaries, it's in precisely this cultural dissonance, says Breyer P-Orridge, that these words of wisdom become all the more powerful.

Text Maxwell Williams  Photography Amy Gwatkin  Styling Samia Giobellina
this page: sketches by Genesis Breyer P-Orridge (2014)  opposite page: organza dress, cotton t-shirt and silk skirt by Yang Li; latex balaclava and long-sleeved top worn underneath by Atsuko Kudo; latex opera gloves by House of Harlot; latex stockings by Kim West

So
Destroy
the
Expected

ANG LI

What Genesis does
is very divisive
— you either like
it or you don't.
When I first came
to London, I was
listening to a
lot of industrial
music, and of
course, Throbbing
Gristle are the
Elvis Presley of
industrial. We met
through Douglas
McCarthy of Nitzer
Ebb. I took a few
days off and flew
to New York and
spent hours just
talking to Gen
before we even
decided to do
anything. It was
very intense at
times. She would
tell me stories
about her past.
It was like she
was spurting out
the noise in her
head, and through
conversation, we
picked things from
both our minds
which complemented
each other, and
thought, 'OK,
what can we make
from that?' If
she was spurting
out the material,
I produced the
record, so
to speak."

GENESIS BREYER
P-ORRIDGE

"How can we wake
people up from
their malaise
of the expected?
This is why it
says 'so destroy
the expected'.
We all fall into
biological and
mental habits.
It's an easy way
for us to navigate
day-to-day work
and life, but it
also doesn't do
us any favours
in terms of
growing into
wisdom, growing
into a greater
understanding of
each other, growing
into a deeper
relationship — all
the things that we
really crave. We
are always looking
for ways to shake
people — not with
shock, but just
with surprise or
novelty or even
a good piece of
wit. Anything
that's unexpected
or mysterious or
curious. Curiosity
is a great weapon
for the artist."

# Laura Jane Grace

## true trans soul rebel

Laura Jane Grace is a force of nature. A daring and individualistic vocalist in Florida punk outfit Against Me! since the late 90s, her fearless blend of the personal and political found new context on last year's album *Transgender Dysphoria Blues*, which explored her transition to living as a woman and ignited conversations not often explored within her band's genre. Yet, speaking on a break from recording a new album in Detroit, Grace insists that her evolution isn't over – far from it.

Text Leonie Cooper  Photography Ryan Lowry

*How old were you when you started to feel trapped in a male body?*

Those feelings were always there for me, from as early as I can remember. But I had never heard the word 'transgender'. The idea and concept of transitioning didn't exist to me.

*What was your reaction to the tragic suicide of Leelah Alcorn, the trans teenager who took her own life in December last year?*

I definitely understand that kind of pain. It's that sense of not being able to see a future with the way you feel, and how to reconcile that with the way society works. That's why transgender visibility is so important – it's about showing young people that it's possible to have a happy adult life. I know how crushing it can be growing up in a small place like that (Alcorn was from Lebanon, Ohio), especially when you don't have the support of your family.

*Leelah wrote 'fix society' in the Tumblr note she left behind – how can that happen?*

It all has to do with education. I find it hard to fault someone if they're uneducated. It's important to break the taboos of gender. Conversion therapy should be made criminal – it's nothing but damaging. When I was in middle school my mother made me go to a church youth group which paid for me to see a therapist and made me feel like something was wrong with me.

*Punk and hardcore are often seen as quite macho and male-dominated genres – is that really the case?*

I think it depends on where you look. I was very much into those British anarcho-peace-punk bands of the 1970s and early 1980s, which had a very strong female presence. That extended over to a lot of things that happened in the Pacific Northwest in the 1990s and the riot grrrl movement. Those were the examples of what I wanted to see in punk. I thought that was a space for me to exist in, because I didn't feel accepted in other places. My friends and I were kind of hippies and we got beat up a lot. So the appeal of punk was the attitude – it was about fighting back and getting angry.

*Do you consider yourself an activist?*

That's definitely very much where I came from. When I got into the Sex Pistols, it was the nihilism that really attracted me, but that only lasted so long. It was the politics behind it that kept me inspired. Then I discovered the punk band Crass and that just changed my life – my first tattoo was a Crass logo when I was 14. The politics I learned from UK anarcho-punk bands are politics I still hold on to today.

*What was your first punk show?*

Green Day – I got into them at the time they were really exploding. It was in Orlando, Florida, at an outdoor venue called The Edge. I went with my best friend. We dyed our hair green with spray-on dye. Because we were all sweaty by the end of the show our skin was totally fucking dyed green. I remember feeling like you had to go into the pit, which was terrifying – I was 13 years old and must have weighed 90lbs. So you went in and you were brutalised and came out knowing you didn't have any fun doing that but then felt like, 'I guess I've got to do that again now!'

*How do you feel about personalities, like Laverne Cox, opening up the conversation, and shows like* Transparent *winning awards – could you have foreseen that five years ago?*

No, not at all! From my experience, seeing other people come out is encouragement to accept myself. Laverne Cox on the cover of *Time* magazine is an example of a positive role model – not the cliché of a Rayon (Jared Leto's character) from *Dallas Buyers Club*. I'd really like to see new clichés, like, 'Oh great, another successful transgender person!'

*Last year, you were vocal in criticising Arcade Fire's 'We Exist' video, which saw Andrew Garfield cast as a transwoman, and then you changed your position. How do you feel about that now?*

Well, first of all I had no idea that a single tweet would ever reach so far! I woke up that morning, drank a cup of coffee, watched a video and made an off-handed remark. I didn't delete it, but talking to Our Lady J (transwoman who coached Garfield in the video) kind of changed my mind – she told me she identified with the experiences in the video. I do still stand by the idea that I wish trans roles would go to trans actors. There's no shortage of transgender actors who can tell their own story.

*You're known for your tattoos, but why did you recently have an entire arm inked black?*

It was a really, really painful eight-hour session in San Francisco. I didn't originally intend to cover up every single tattoo, but once they started one thing led to another. To be able to wipe the slate clean is oddly refreshing. It's black now, but the black will fade, and I'll be able to tattoo on to the black. I don't ever want to stop shape-shifting.

*You're currently working on your seventh album. What can we expect?*

I felt a real burst of creativity towards the end of the year. At first it was a little bit hard to wrap my head around what direction to go in. Our last record was very personal and pretty heavy for me. So it's not like you're going to take the approach of, 'So this record's even more personal!' I think I just wanted to write a record that's really fun. It's fun songs to listen and dance to and hopefully that'll translate for everyone.

*You're also writing your autobiography – how's that going?*

It's kind of like *Get in the Van* (Henry Rollins' 1994 memoir of his years in Black Flag), but a little more transsexual.

# Lady Bunny
## my obsession: beefcakes

Lady Bunny has a penchant for pecs. Since sending shockwaves through the 80s gay club scene with her Barbra-on-barbiturates mile-high blonde wig, she's been an unstoppable, fabulous firecracker. To celebrate the release of new book *Beefcake*, the dean of drag sounds off about the greased-up, sculpted sort of butch she loves to drool over.

"What turns you on is what turns you on. There is something so appealing about seeing a Greek god with short hair slicked back or an 1800s cowboy with the classic, clean-cut side part and heavy bangs that were so popular in the 1960s. I don't know if you've noticed, but male Hollywood A-list stars usually aren't hot any more. Nicolas Cage, Bruce Willis and Tom Hanks might have the everyman appeal of a Jimmy Stewart, but they don't exactly make you cream your jeans and rewind that VHS to rewatch the parts of their films in which they disrobe. If you are turned on by manly men, who is more manly than young straight men? They're some of the most sizzling homoerotic images of all time."

Text Trey Taylor
all images taken from Beefcake: 100% Rare, All-Natural, All-American, out in April via Rizzoli

**INTERNATIONAL STÜSSY TRIBE**

LOS ANGELES · SPRING 2015 BY TYRONE LEBON

# Jim Shaw
## my obsession: trashy paintings

Cult artist and former Destroy All Monsters punk Jim Shaw has been trawling through America's cultural scrapheap since the 70s. For the Barbican's new exhibition, *Magnificent Obsessions: The Artist as Collector*, Shaw brings his thrift store paintings and assortment of ghoulish oddities across the Atlantic so others can celebrate his love affair with junk.

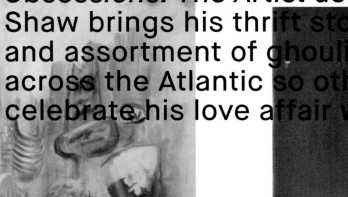

"My older cousin exposed me to the wonders of comic books, then monster magazines, which became a quiet outlet for the aggression and sadism that are normally tossed against society by ten-year-old boys. This developed into collecting these paintings. I'm looking for things that say something about the underside of American culture. The weirder the better, and if it's some adolescent version of surrealism, even more so. I seem to sniff out the apocalyptic in the world, but I'm also a cheery optimist. While my collection is often humorous on the surface, I hope it has a sad or sinister aspect trailing off it."

Text Dominique Sisley
all images taken from Magnificent Obsessions: The Artist as Collector, which runs at Barbican Art Gallery, London, until May 25

# STEVE MADDEN

## The Haxan Cloak
## my obsession:
## heartbreak songs

Wielding blackened, fuzz-heavy synths and doomy, disorientating bass, producer Bobby Krlic AKA The Haxan Cloak offers up the kind of anguish best served through a huge, pounding speaker. Brought up on a diet of "heartbreak music" from Roy Orbison to Joy Division, Krlic recently worked on Björk's new album *Vulnicura*, which gut-wrenchingly explores the breakdown of her own relationship.

GLUE WINGS ONTO FLOWERS THERE,
AND FEED THOSE FLOWERS TO THAT HORSE.
GIVE ALL THE PIGEONS NAMES,
UNTIL THEY FLY AWAY,
AND THEN
GLUE WINGS ONTO FLOWERS
ALL OVER AGAIN.

"It's a feeling that's absolutely universal, yet every time you're heartbroken it's completely unique. Songs on that subject matter are very well crafted. They come from a pure place. My dad always used to say that sometimes you can find great comfort in discomfort. I can really identify with that. It's like watching a horror film and you know you're not going to be able to sleep but you want to watch it anyway."

Text Daisy Jones
images clockwise from top right: Roy Orbison, Crying (1962); Thee Silver Mt. Zion Memorial Orchestra & Tra-La-La Band, Horses in the Sky (2005); Joy Division, Love Will Tear Us Apart (1980)

# INCLUSIVE INSURANCE
## THAT'S SAVVY CHIC

Bianca J thought a brand new Fiat 500 was out of her league, let alone having to pay extra for pricey insurance. Well, she was glad to be wrong. She chose a Fiat 500 with i-Deal powered by Carrot Insurance. It's one of the best ways of getting behind the wheel. With Fiat i-Deal powered by Carrot, Bianca gets fixed monthly payments covering PCP finance*, insurance▲ and servicing†, and can even get cash rewards for being a good driver. And a Smartphone app to help her keep tabs on her driving style. To find out how you can get this season's must have Fiat 500 at an equally must have price, visit www.fiat500withinsurance.co.uk

### OWN • INSURE • SERVICE
### THAT'S i-DEAL

Fiat with **EXPO** MILANO 2015

FIAT

fiat.co.uk

# My Love Don't Cost a Thing
## by andrew durbin

He photographed himself in a bathtub full of little slices of cucumbers, some of which he placed under his soaked white t-shirt like strange nipples. There's something almost puritanical in how the white tub, white t-shirt, and green vegetables have been linked together on my narrow iPhone screen in spare form, charged by some singular force that arrives in reverence for transcendence of flesh via the various systems of information exchange that carry his image to me. According to the geotag feature on Instagram, he's based in south-east London, somewhere near Goldsmiths, though only one photograph indicates where he was when he took it, so he could be anywhere for that matter. He could still be in the tub, adrift in the lazy mist of cucumber water, hand poised overhead to selfie the moment into the cloud. When I show his picture to Kevin, Kevin says, "I think he's a J.W.Anderson model." "Definitely not," I say. I keep tagging Kevin in his photos to see if we can get his attention, but nothing comes of it. Like, flirtations without the real, there's nothing to be had except some dumb semblance of sex in the heady air of my feed, whatever that might mean. I do actually get kind of hard at the thought of him in London looking at Instagram, wondering who I might be, in New York, tagging someone named Kevin, also in New York. Or hardness isn't the word so much as it's a dowsing sense of a person who couldn't care less and as such lingers at the magnetic zero-point of some entropic bliss that places me in front of the mirror, thinking about him and checking myself out to see why my body isn't as nice as his. We are not the same. I put on a white shirt and get into the tub with my phone. Everything must eventually get out of hand.

Andrew Durbin is a poet and editor based in New York City. His latest collection of poetry, Mature Themes, riffs on subjects from Katy Perry and the meaning of tracksuits to the frontiers of network consciousness. He is currently working on a novel about cults.

# AnOther

Brand new **anothermag.com**,
coming soon. Your modern guide
to fashion, culture & ideas.

From hood rat to heroine, Yo-landi Visser has led a life of extremes.
As the Die Antwoord frontwoman prepares to take on Hollywood
with *Chappie*, she lets Caroline Ryder in on her unpredictable rise to fame

# Dark Star

photography Pierre Debusschere    styling Robbie Spencer

Yo-landi Visser appears in the piano bar of an old-school west Hollywood hotel, looking like an albino gangster from another dimension. Wearing a sweater bearing the legend 'BO$$' in large green letters across the front, the Die Antwoord frontwoman perches on a leather armchair and orders coffee and fresh fruit. Guests sneak glances at her, no doubt wondering where this fragile-yet-formidable life form with a silvery white mullet, corresponding eyebrows and little-girl voice sprang from. "I roll with bodyguards when I go back home to South Africa," she says, looking around the room. "Like, full-on. People want to fucking assassinate me." It's hard to imagine this five-foot tall mother of two should pose such a threat to the self-proclaimed torchbearers of decency and good taste in society. But that's what happens when misfits succeed. Feathers get ruffled.

Visser, real name Anri du Toit, has fast become an unlikely pop-culture icon. Flipping between Lolita songbird vocals and thugged-out raps delivered in a blend of English and Afrikaans, she has broken every approved music industry convention en route to success with her bandmates, rapper Ninja and DJ Hi-Tek. Since exploding on the scene in 2010 with their viral video "Enter the Ninja", Die Antwoord have compromised their vision for nobody, aiming to remain as "punk and fresh and kind of psycho" as possible. At the end of last year they confirmed their A-list clout with the cameo-heavy video for "Ugly Boy", with appearances by Jack Black, Marilyn Manson, Flea, the ATL Twins, an almost topless Dita Von Teese, and supermodel Cara Delevingne. Cheered on by the obsessive freaks and geeks that have claimed Die Antwoord as their own, they have become one of the world's most visceral live acts, with crowds proclaiming their allegiance by chanting "zef, zef, zef" – an homage to the downwardly mobile South African street culture that inspired their favourite band's trashy aesthetic.

Visser rarely grants interviews, and never solo interviews – until now. She prefers to remain an enigma; an elfin rave avatar whose life story remains relatively undiscussed. "I got irritated with people asking us the same questions," she says. "Like, 'Are you a real band?' Journalists wanted to slay us, tried to cut us down, and I just started caring less and less about doing interviews. With Facebook and Instagram, you kind of don't need to anyway. But now and again we'll do something when there's new information to share. Like now."

After amassing more than 200 million views on their YouTube channels, the group will make the leap on to the big screen next month when Visser and Ninja star alongside Sigourney Weaver and Hugh Jackman in *Chappie*, a family sci-fi drama by *District 9* director Neill Blomkamp. In the film, they play a pair of musicians-turned-gangsters who adopt a newborn artificial intelligence in the shape of a robot, Chappie. "There's something about Yo-landi and Ninja, they both have very unusual magnetism," says Blomkamp over the phone during a break from editing the film. "Whether you love them or you don't, you're drawn to them. Yo-landi has something that is hard to put into words. There's some unknown factor about her that just makes you interested. She has this split personality – the dichotomy between the imagery you see and the lyrics she is singing is fascinating. That, coupled with the fact that she is actually very smart, makes people identify with her in a different way to anyone else."

Born on March 3, 1984 in Port Alfred, a small town on South Africa's east coast, Visser was adopted by a priest and his wife and struggled to feel like she belonged anywhere. Growing up, she describes herself as "a little punk" who was always getting into fistfights. "Which is weird, because actually I am quite soft and caring." She considered herself goth in spirit ("me and my best friend even dyed our underwear black in the bath") and obsessed over Nirvana, PJ Harvey, Nine Inch Nails, Cypress Hill, Eminem, Marilyn Manson and Aphex Twin. "I loved dark shit. When the Chris Cunningham video for (Aphex Twin's) 'Come to Daddy' came out, that was like a fucking religion." It's an influence that's plainly felt in the dark yet wry, blood-splattered video for "Ugly Boy", which features Visser as a cute but terrifying alien being with eyes as black as night. Fittingly, the song is actually a refix of Aphex's 1992 track, "Ageispolis".

At 16, Visser was sent to a boarding school nine hours' drive from her family home, where, surrounded by other creative kids, she finally blossomed. "The school was very artistic and open-minded for South Africa," she says. "I was fucking happy. For the first time in my life, I connected with people who were artistic." She has never met her birth parents, and she doesn't want to now. She doesn't know too much about them, except that her mother was white. Recently, a portrait artist specialising in identifying genetic history told Visser she has the facial structure of a 'coloured' (in South Africa, 'coloured' is the commonly used term for mixed race). At first, Visser was confused. "I said, 'No, I'm white.' She kept asking about my family and then I started thinking maybe I am coloured." Visser now thinks her father may have been black. She was born during apartheid, and believes her white mother's parents may have forced her to give her baby up for adoption, after getting pregnant by a black guy. It's a theory.

Another determining factor in Visser's identity has been Ninja, father of her daughter, and her sparring partner in Die Antwoord. "We're bound by life and music. One doesn't work without the other." Ninja, real name Watkin Tudor Jones, 40, had been on the South African hip hop scene since age 13. He grew up in Johannesburg and frequented black nightclubs where he cut

"I love dark shit. When the video for Aphex Twin's 'Come to Daddy' came out, that was like a fucking religion"

previous spread
cotton knickers by Nude Label

this page
puffa jacket by Cottweiler

latex hooded top by Cottweiler; trainers
Yo-landi's own

his teeth as a rapper. "You had to be good to do that shit," says Visser. "The fact that he was white meant he had to be *really* good." Visser met Ninja outside a Cape Town club around 2003. He was sporting a similar suited-and-booted attire to slick hip hop duo Handsome Boy Modeling School. "She was like, 'What the fuck's up with this dude?'" recalls Ninja. "Why are you dressed like that? Don't speak to me.' She was a little goth kid who looked about 13. I was scared of her."

After reconnecting at one of his own shows, Ninja asked the gothy Visser to lend vocals to a track by his horrorcore act, The Constructus Corporation. "I just wanted her to go 'yeah motherfucker' with an American accent," he says. "We went into the studio and she did it with this attitude and her voice. I was just like, 'ARGH!'" Visser told him she didn't know anything about rap, and he promised to teach her. They became romantically involved for a period, and in 2006, she got pregnant by Ninja.

"I was young," she says. "I was like, 'Fuck, my life is over,' because all my friends were out smoking weed and hanging out and hood-ratting, and I was at home with the baby. But I was psycho about it. No smoking and drinking. I wanted to be a cool mom. It was hectic. I felt very isolated for a long time but in the end it was cool, because it helped me and Ninja stick together. If we hadn't, we would have maybe drifted." Though they are no longer a couple (Ninja is now married), many fans continue to assume they're an item. "A lot of people still see us as a couple," says Visser. "I understand – we have such a unique companionship, it's really weird that we're not. But it's hard being in a group together and having a kid."

Ninja and Visser's daughter, Sixteen Jones, is currently in a band with Flea's daughter, Sunny, called The Boy With the Rainbow Face. "Sunny is the lead and Sixteen is the backup and writer," says Visser, who's lived in LA for the past few years. "She's really good." In keeping with rebellious-kid tradition, Sixteen is the opposite of her parents in that she can't stand foul language.

Visser is also a parent to Tokkie, a street kid she adopted four years ago. He was nine years old at the time, from a rough neighbourhood in Jo'burg. His family was poor, so Visser offered to take care of him at weekends, and then full-time. "I've always had that maternal thing; that connection with street kids and people who are misfits," says Visser. "I saw so much potential in Tokkie but I knew there was no hope for him on the street. No one's gonna give a shit. Now he's blossomed and become this enchanting boy."

In 2007, Visser suggested the idea of starting a group to Ninja, and the seeds of Die Antwoord were sown. While working on new tracks, they met Hi-Tek, their third member

and DJ. "Something just happened," she says. "A triangle. But we wanted to have a real look. Not just go in the studio and make some songs. We wanted to have a whole style." This is where the hair comes in.

Visser swears it wasn't until she started sporting her brutal, cyber-punky peroxide mullet that Die Antwoord really found its visual direction. It was 2009, and they were shooting a video. The director wanted her to be all little-girl and cutesy. "My hair was long with a fringe and people would make jokes, calling me Britney and Lady Gaga. I told Ninja I needed to go in a different fucking direction. I wanted to have an edge that was more like me on the inside. Ninja said we should just cut the sides off, and I said, 'Fuck, let's do it.' And it was just, BAM – there's Yo-landi. It affected the music, it affected the way I acted and how I felt. For me it was like a birth or something." Visser's haircut and bleached eyebrows represent more than a fashion quirk or a cry for attention. They are a statement of her outsider pride; an unmissable declaration of who she is and what she stands for. Ninja still cuts her hair to this day. No one else is allowed to touch it.

Cool hair or not, no-one gave a shit about Die Antwoord. They had two songs out, and an album, *$O$*. They'd made a video for "Enter the Ninja" that featured Visser as a cyberpunk schoolgirl heroine, wearing underwear with marker-emblazoned dollar signs, and a rat crawling over her. Her image flipped the Lolita archetype on its head, with body language that screamed, "Look, but don't fucking touch." She may have been dressed like a schoolgirl, but unlike Britney and her entreaties to 'hit me baby one more time', Visser's attire was more a method of visual torture, double-daring the viewer to underestimate her strength.

Visser remembers the night everything changed as if it was yesterday. It was February 3, 2010, and they had been booked to play a show in Johannesburg. "It was raining, and I was saying to Ninja, 'Fuck, no one's coming because of the rain. We drove around the corner and saw kids queuing around the block. And as we walked up, people started screaming. I remember rapping that night; the mics were fucked and the crowd rapped all our lyrics. I remember going home and wondering what the fuck had just happened. It was like something aligned. All the kids connected with this thing that we were feeling."

That night, their video got 10,000 new hits. Their email address was still on their website and the fan messages started pouring in. The following morning, their video was featured on US television, and a day or two after that, someone from Interscope got hold of their phone number. They flew to the States for a meeting with legendary label head Jimmy Iovine at Interscope HQ. "We walked into the offices and saw NWA, Slim Shady and Tupac on the wall. I was like, 'Fuck, this is the best label.'

"I wanted to be a cool mom. It was hectic. I felt very isolated for a long time"

We were like these wild animals from South Africa in a meeting with Jimmy Iovine. He said, 'We love you guys, we don't want you to change a thing.'" So after a couple months' thinking time, they signed with the label and got ready for their first US show, at Coachella. It became the most buzzed-about performance of the festival.

Soon enough, Hollywood came knocking. In 2010, David Fincher reached out to Visser about playing the lead in his adaptation of *The Girl With the Dragon Tattoo*. "Ari (Emanuel, Visser's agent) was calling me saying, 'You have to take this role or your career is over,'" she says. "But I said no. For me with music, there is no half-stepping. This is my calling." Visser felt that, if she stepped away from music for a year or two to make a movie, Die Antwoord would lose focus. Fincher kept asking to meet with her, and she kept refusing. "I always make a decision, even if it's the wrong one. I hate being confused. I'm like, 'Fuck it, I am going in this direction, and I am going hard.'"

At the same time, Ninja was considering a film offer from Neill Blomkamp to star in *Elysium*. "I told him, 'No, I don't think it's right,' and we had a big fight," says Visser. "Ninja is super-ambitious, more than I am. He's like, 'Let's do everything.' But I felt like if his attention was distracted for a year, we'd be fucked. I said, 'Let's wait.'" The role went to Matt Damon, and the pair went back to South Africa to work on their second album with DJ Hi-Tek.

They delivered the record, *Ten$ion*, to Interscope and waited to hear back. "It was like fucking school," says Visser. "They said, 'Well, it's good, but it needs more rave.' We were like, 'How much more rave do you want?'" The label told them they needed to write three more songs, including a collaboration with a commercial artist. "We were like, 'Fuck you! Why should we collaborate?' We should only do that if we really dig someone, like when you're hanging tough and it just works. There was this weird pressure. So we called our lawyer and said, 'Can you make Interscope go away?'"

Their lawyer wasn't sure how easy it would be. "It was like a fucking bible, the contract we had signed with them." Luckily for the group, Interscope let Die Antwoord go without much of a fight. "I think they were scared of Ninja, to be honest. They had wired us $1 million, so we wired it back. We didn't want the money. It was more important to us to make something we believed in. Everyone was saying, 'They are a fucking joke band, they are fake.' I was like, 'No, we really wanna get better and prove that we didn't just get lucky like Vanilla Ice.' We wanted to prove that we are going to make music until we die." In 2012, the following year, the band released *Ten$ion* on their own label, Zef Recordz, and declined an offer from Lady Gaga to open up on the South African leg of her tour.

Currently, they're working on a fourth album with DJ Muggs of Cypress Hill after meeting him at a *quinceañera*, a traditional Mexican birthday party, in the heavily Latino neighbourhood of East LA. "Me and Ninja roll up and it was like the fucking *Godfather*, low-riders and suits and wives and I was like, 'What the fuck?' A friend introduced us to Muggs. We had always loved that dark shit. Cypress had those beats that were so warm and cosy and dark and hard. Instantly we clicked and Ninja said that night, 'We have to do it with him.'" So far they have eight songs, recorded at Muggs' studio and another place owned by Flea, both in LA. The tracks, says Visser, are "fucking insane and dark and epic and moody and just phat. I always joke with Muggs that he is the same breed as us. We dig the same things and for me, that's what I meant about collaborations feeling right."

Their collaboration with Blomkamp for *Chappie* felt similarly organic. Rather than trying to shape them to fit his vision, the South African director used the pair's existing personas as the springboard for his script. He wanted them to play themselves in a world of his creation. "I look around and I see a lot of artists every day, and not many of them are actually doing what their heart is telling them to do," says Blomkamp. "The artists we are exposed to in mass media tend to be very watered-down and predictable. Yo-landi and Ninja are not influenced by the external forces that derail most artists and make them put out very benign, boring work. I think that is by far the most interesting and refreshing thing about them." Despite initially doubting whether a global audience would understand the pair's accents, the executives financing the movie sided with Blomkamp's insistence that it was impossible to make the project with anyone else.

While filming *Chappie*, some of the movie's producers finally recognised Visser and Ninja's on-screen magnetism, and said they wanted to make a TV show about them – scripted or reality, whatever they wanted. At the time, Visser and Ninja had already started work on a film in South Africa documenting their life story, but they decided a TV show would afford them more latitude to tell their story. "We wanted to do it about the real shit that happened. How we signed to Interscope. About the night we blew up. About our kid. About the wild-wild-west adventures we have had. You can't make shit like that up – it's almost supernatural. There's never a dull moment. It's always fucking something." They plan to call the show *ZEF*. In fact, Visser says they are even considering changing the band's name to Zef. "Fucking Die Antwoord... I mean, it's cool because it sounds hard and German and has this cool meaning that is like the essence for us. 'The answer'. I have a tenderness for it. But Zef is just like, easy. Ninja's fucking easy. Yo-landi's fucking easy. And Zef is fucking easy. Let's see, eh?"

"Interscope wired us $1 million, so we wired it back. We didn't want the money"

hair Shon at Julian Watson Agency; make-up Isamaya Ffrench at Streeters using M.A.C; nails Kate Cutler using WAH London; photographic assistants Ismaël Moumin, Samuel Hearn; styling assistants Lizy Curtis, Laura Page; hair assistant Ryuta Saiga; make-up assistant Josh Wilks; digital operator Francesco de la Porta; special thanks to Spring Studios London

164

Ninja, Yo-landi's partner-in-rhyme, has dragged listeners to hell and back with his psychotic verses and intense stage presence. He gives Owen Myers his six commandments to live by

# Zef Master

## I
### Uncensor yourself
Jung had this thing he defined as the 'shadow self': the self that thinks some fucked-up shit that you can't say. That's both of us when we are fucking with Die Antwoord. I started taking my filters away and saying whatever the fuck I thought. We transformed into these new, hyper versions of ourselves. I don't even remember who I was before.

## II
### Free your mind
It's weird, me and Yo-landi are like this one thing. I know what she's thinking sometimes, like identical twins. As a couple it would be too limiting. You have your jealousy and insecurity, and we just went past that into this hive-mind stage.

## III
### Push the limits
At our first shows, people would come and stand around and talk and drink like they were used to doing. And that's the wrong shit. Yo-landi would snap and push motherfuckers to make them stop talking. If you're not down with this, don't come to our show or you're gonna get slammed.

## IV
### Adopt a robot
It's like this dysfunctional family film where our kids are robots. It's super-personal in a way: it's cute as fuck and dope and it's just quite intimate. Neill (Blomkamp) was super-specific: '(Imagine) it's 2016 and your music career has failed so you're fucking dealing drugs.'

## V
### Start a movement
Zef is the blackest joke. It was an insult made up by non-zef people; it was like talking shit about people – 'Eurgh, that dress is so zef, it's disgusting.' Yo-landi just started swearing so bad and saying, 'We zef,' which is like saying, 'I'm a piece-of-shit scumbag, I'm that person you hate, I'm that thing you're embarrassed about.' We made it into a fucking movement.

## VI
### Go with the flow
Yo-landi has got better. She can rhyme now; she flows. We write for each other – she'll write a verse for me and say, 'You should say this shit.' She's like this little disciple that overtook the master.

Comme des Garçons' killer SS15 show was an operatic musing on love,
lust, life and death – as represented by the colour red.
Isabella Burley marvels at the power of Rei Kawakubo's vision

# War of the Roses

photography Jeff Bark    styling Robbie Spencer

In a season defined by an obsession with placid beauty, Rei Kawakubo – one of fashion's most defiant and cryptic figures – hit us with a collection that raged violently against the surface level. Inside a derelict warehouse in Paris, she sent out an aggressive procession of explosive silhouettes rendered in an overwhelming, all-red colour palette. Red has always been a powerful signifier, but in the hands of the Comme des Garçons figurehead, its conflicting associations with rage, suffering, love, lust, life and death all came into emotional consciousness.

Kawakubo's signature is to create clothes that demand an extreme reaction, but this season's show felt powerfully unnerving, set to a jarring soundtrack curated by Frédéric Sanchez featuring drone metal bands such as Earth and Sunn O))). "With Comme des Garçons it's different because Rei doesn't tell you about a theme," says Sanchez. "What was interesting – and something I hadn't experienced in a long time – was that she really wanted me to *look* at the clothes very intensely beforehand. The moment I saw the collection, violent and emotional images came into my head. I thought of Derek Jarman movies, like *The Last of England*, and the Countess Elizabeth Báthory (the infamous female serial killer known for bathing in her victims' blood). It was violent and passionate, but without the feeling of horror. The final idea was to do something subtle. Something that felt like no music, but which filled the space."

Backstage, the notoriously elusive designer gave the words 'roses' and 'blood' as her explanation for the show. It was an interesting pairing: two disparate ideas that came together in this most conflicted of collections. "There was something almost operatic and theatrical because of the red," says Sanchez. "It gave a feeling of unreality, while also expressing something about the violent world we live in at the moment. It's not real, but it is – that's what makes it so special." For Kawakubo, clothes alone have never told the whole story. What she achieved this season was to trigger an emotional response that stayed with us, reverberating far beyond the catwalk. Fashion could do with more of that.

all clothes and accessories Comme des Garçons SS15

hair Shingo Shibata at The Wall Group using Rodin by Recine Luxury Hair Oil; make-up Francelle at Art + Commerce; models Molly Bair and Harleth Kuusik at The Society Management; photographic assistants Chris White, Michael Casker, Matt Munson; styling assistants Victor Cordero, Lizy Curtis; hair assistant Shuhei Kadowaki; make-up assistant Mami Iizuka; casting Noah Shelley

Fashion collectives Eckhaus Latta and Gypsy Sport are hot-wiring NYC's downtown scene. Trey Taylor and Antwaun Sargent tune in to their utopian vision

# Wanna Be in Our Gang?

photography Rachel Chandler   styling Tom Guinness

previous spread and this spread
all clothes and accessories by Eckhaus Latta

models in order of appearance: Thor Shannon, Caroline Noona, Alexandra Marzella, Jasper Briggs, Lenka Ouchi Latocha, Mari Ouchi, Lilac Cianciolo

Cruising by the familiar posters and billboard ads generously plastered around lower Manhattan, you might be shocked when confronted with a row of images depicting a young boy in a white mesh tee huffing poppers. The small brown bottle, cosying up to his right nostril, bore the label 'Eckhaus Latta Sport'. "Our friends that were on their way to work would be getting off the subway and texting us pictures like, 'What the fuck?!'" laughs LA-based Zoe Latta, one half of bicoastal design duo Eckhaus Latta. "It was definitely the most physically overt thing we've done," chimes in her creative partner, Mike Eckhaus, from his studio in New York. The billboards, which the pair insist were not "meant to shock", were created with artist Bjarne Melgaard to advertise a gallery show at Gavin Brown's Enterprise called *Ignorant Transparencies*. To complement the posters (ripped down just 24 hours after they were illegally put up), Eckhaus Latta created a shrinkwrap 'cosmetics sex kit' including a condom, poppers and lube.

If this sounds at all strange to you, then their SS15 collection might just send you flying off the handle. There were bum-grazing low-rise dresses and flirty tank tops revealing chest hair, sexless jeans, teddy bear terrycloth shorts, and gym-class socks painted on legs. Dirty sneakers were even stacked on top of each other to create their own unique hybrid. "Those were a collaboration with our friend Misha Kahn," explains Eckhaus. Kahn, a product designer and artist, was at a gallery opening, and wore the shoes as "a joke... I think! We were dying over that. We both said, 'We *have* to work with you for our next show.' I think the shoes he wore were actually in the show." Even more unorthodox than their designs was the

rotating cast they were featured on. Confounding expectations, they cast a mix of friends including transgender actress Hari Nef, reblog-ready artists Mike Bailey-Gates and India Salvor Menuez, and elderly models from Central Casting for the collection. To the tune of a live backing choir, they were trumpeting their message from on high: "A person is really what makes the clothing," says Eckhaus. Call their casting transgressive if you like – they prefer the term 'inclusive'. "This is about people who feel good and

"This is about people who feel good and confident with their bodies" Mike Eckhaus

confident with their bodies, which is something that I feel is universal amongst genders and sexes, ages and races," says Eckhaus. "It's very important to us when we're considering how we're going to present our clothing."

The pair met in their senior year studying at the Rhode Island School of Design. Apparently, Eckhaus didn't warm to his classmate Latta from the outset. "We didn't really like each other initially, for reasons that don't make sense now," he laughs. "We just didn't

know each other." It was only when Eckhaus put on a flea market sale and Latta asked to see his closet that the idea to join forces began to germinate. "We became obsessed with each other," he continues, quickly adding, "but we are very different people." Latta finishes: "I think that's why it works."

Since then, the pair have proved to be prolific collaborators, teaming up to work with documentary filmmaker Alexa Karolinski ("She's deeply part of the family"), contemporary artist and runway-floor pioneer Alex Da Corte ("The room man. He knows how to sell the room"), visual artist Alexandra Marzella AKA @artwerk6666 ("Her presence is so amazing, I haven't seen it in many people"), and a major market-index of young, cool New York creatives.

Now they're pulling up their gym-class socks in the hope of making it into the big leagues. "There's this American paint company called Sherwin-Williams," says Latta. "Its disgusting logo is a picture of the globe covered in paint with the words, 'Cover the Earth' – that's their mantra. At the end of the day when you're producing things, the nicest thing is the feeling of spreading the seed or distributing it. And it's slowly happening for us, but it's this human feeling of having the gratification of seeing people wear these things." With a nascent brand teetering on the edge of mainstream success, the duo simply hopes that their message gets across, whether that recipient is six years old or 60. Plan B? Selling poppers. TT

When Gypsy Sport staged an illegal fashion show at Washington Square Park – locus of the recent Millions March – in September of last year, they weren't just choosing an unconventional location, they were aligning themselves with New York's most storied site of resistance. As crowds gathered around a concrete catwalk, models emerged wearing necklaces made of yellow public transit cards, futuristic do-rags and colourful crop tops – all reminiscent of the genderfuck movement of the 1970s.

"We didn't want a traditional runway show – that's not Gypsy Sport," explains creative director Rio Uribe. "Our brand is all about being on the street every day." With no permit, the guerilla event confirmed the brand's message of nonconformity (they even let the models choose what they wanted to wear) and quickly became one of the most-hyped shows at New York Fashion Week SS15.

Known for infusing their Harlem roots with global culture, Uribe and design partner Jerome Williams are set on disrupting our collective sense of style by forcing us to explore cultural references and achieve a kind of aesthetic liberation. "Artistically, we are the Indigo Era between streetwear and high fashion," says Williams, who likes to "throw some beads on that bitch" when Uribe's designs aren't living up to the label's culture-vulture outlook. "Our message is to show global awareness through our clothes. Not everyone is going to get it, but we are building something here."

Now into their fourth season, Gypsy Sport have infiltrated New York's downtown scene, recruiting everyone from A$AP Ferg to underground club culture's steamiest new voice Lafawndah

(who featured in their Bollywood-inspired AW14 fashion film). But already their world extends far beyond the five boroughs. Last year, they were invited to create custom accessories – think visor hats and face-protectors – for *The Hunger Games: Mockingjay* parts one and two. "Being young in NYC is like being in *The Hunger Games*," laughs Uribe. "Competition is alive and well here. I was overwhelmed when we were approached. My little sister and I had just finished reading the books,

so the story was fresh in my mind. I thought my reply to them was too long and enthusiastic, but it worked."

The experience may have drawn them into a terrifying cinematic universe, but the designers, who have known each other for more than a decade, are much more interested in creating their own utopian reality. They've even got a name for it: 'Haturn', a mythical place representing what Uribe describes as their "don't-give-a-fuck attitude". The name has since become

their logo, taking the physical form of two hats upside down; an ode to their roots as a hat label.

For their SS15 campaign, titled Bromance, Uribe and Williams took us on a long train ride from Harlem to the Rockaways (via Haturn), fully aware that it's illegal to film on New York public transit. "I did my research," says Uribe. "I knew we couldn't get arrested, we just had to run when they spotted us on the train." But subway car-jumping isn't all they've done to stir up controversy. This season, they dreamed up something even more provocative – a Gypsy burka. For them, the garment represents cultural awareness. "I don't think it's shocking at all. I think it's beautiful," says Williams. "A lot of people are scared of Muslims right now. I just want people to know that all people, no matter what their religious beliefs, are accepted."

Gypsy Sport might not be the only brand to draw inspiration from unlikely places, but with its irreverent approach to cultural diversity, it might be one of the most progressive ("It's a balance of world culture and city culture," says Uribe of their aesthetic). Asked what he's dreaming up next, Uribe cites *Clueless* and, bizarrely, the fact that "these rugby polo shirts go all over the world after they go out of style in the US" as having piqued his interest lately. So, next up? Clueless in Cambodia. AS

"Being young in NYC is like being in *The Hunger Games*" Rio Uribe

this spread
all clothes and accessories by Gypsy Sport

models in order of appearance: Estelle Atam,
Lafawndah, Ducati Mist, Abiah Hostvedt,
Abby; grooming throughout Ingeborg
at OPUS Beauty using Leonor Greyl and
Sisley Paris; photographic assistant
Butch Hogan

Marilyn Manson is back and he's itching for a fight.
Tim Noakes meets him to talk guns, porn and
why we're all coming back as zombies with hard-ons

A Nose for Trouble

photography Jeff Henrikson    styling Emma Wyman

Apart from the darkness, it's the sound of icy rain tapping against the hotel suite's windows that you notice first. Then the murder-black bin bags taped over the doors. Then the sub-zero air conditioning. Edging further in, flickering candles illuminate the silhouette of the room's sole inhabitant – Marilyn Manson; Antichrist Superstar, Omēga, the God of Fuck. Settled in the corner on a beige sofa, his face is characteristically pasty, but it's too dark to see if he's wearing those infamous off-centre contact lenses or not. Close up, he looks like a beefy, six-foot Nosferatu with a Third Reich haircut.

Following in the footsteps of Alice Cooper, Manson is the quintessential American Frankenstein. Fusing a Hollywood icon and a murderous cult leader for his nom de plume, he revels in holding a mirror up to the world and showing how beautifully ugly it can be. There's no denying that, since he released *Portrait of an American Family* in 1994, the singer has made the shadows a more interesting place to roam. Satirising and subverting imagery of popes, porn stars and pop idols, he has sold 68 million records, turned dancefloor classics "Tainted Love" and "Sweet Dreams (Are Made of This)" into electro-goth anthems, and most recently reinvented himself on the small screen as a gay white supremacist in *Sons of Anarchy*. He's also found time to model for Saint Laurent, marry and divorce Dita Von Teese, and charm the likes of Traci Lords, Stoya and Jenna Jameson (but insists he never watches skin flicks to look for potential dates).

In January, Manson released *The Pale Emperor*, a blues-influenced desert rock opus that is his best work since the alien androgyny of 1998's *Mechanical Animals*. It was recorded during his mother's last months and is, as you'd expect under the circumstances, his most introspective album to date. Still, there's plenty of time for classic Manson missives on sin and sex ("Deep Six"), drugs ("Third Day of a Seven Day Binge") and guns – lots of guns. The influence of firearm culture weighs heavily on the album, which opens with "Killing Strangers" and revisits the theme on "Cupid Carries a Gun". It may be 16 years since the media made him a scapegoat for the Columbine High School massacre – the teenage shooters idolised him and his music – but the scars are still raw.

While his 90s rock peers flounder in the internet era, Manson's influence shows no sign of abating – he recently popped up for a cameo in Die Antwoord's "Ugly Boy" video, symbolically passing the torch to Yo-landi Visser. So what is this all-American bogeyman's secret to everlasting success? "A Faustian deal with the devil," he says with a wicked smile as the candlelight dances across his pallid skin. "I've been hearing the hellhounds knocking at my door for a long time now. I finally realised it's time for me to pay back what I owe, and that's this record. Pay the devil's due."

*You were a music journalist before starting your own band. Did you script the mythology of Marilyn Manson's life first and then bend reality to fit?*
No, it was all very much off the hip. I just dealt with shit as it came along. Like, if some zombies came in here right now, what are we gonna do? My beer bottle would be a useful ghetto knife. You've got a pen, you could write a suicide letter or stab someone in the throat or kill yourself. The point is, I like the idea of improvising, of restricting myself. That is why I prefer club shows to festivals. It's annoying to have to fucking prance back and forth so far. It's not out of laziness; it just doesn't have the intimacy or the energy of a club show. People love to see a club show because they can feel the power. They can smell you.

*Last year you did a club show and invited Johnny Depp and Ninja from Die Antwoord on stage to play 'The Beautiful People'. What are your memories of that night?*
Someone ripped my vest and I brained them. I use the word 'brained' because I think it's very antiquated. I didn't know at the time if it was a guy or girl but I found out later that it was someone from the female genus with my fist imprinted on their forehead. I apologised by kissing her on the hand and laughing at my fist-print on her forehead. The show was very visceral – there were no barricades, there were no bodyguards, there was no security. It was also on Halloween, which is my least favourite holiday, because what am I supposed to dress up as? Me?

*To conservatives, you represent the American nightmare. But what scares you about the States?*
That's hard to say. At one point I considered becoming an ex-patriot and disowning America, but then I decided that America needed me to be a prick in its side, the thorn in the finger. I didn't pay attention in history class, I barely went to school and it surprises me that I graduated, but I think it's very strange that a few people from England went to another continent,

created a book of rules and everyone believes it's right! And now America has to stick their dick and their nose in every goddamn thing across the world and they somehow believe that it's righteous or political when it's simply financial. I mean, that's the sad fact of finding out ignorance is bliss, when you find out that you can't change the world. I can barely change my pants.

*Your extreme stage persona and oration skills have earned you comparisons with the Pope and Adolf Hitler. Which do you feel the most kinship with?*
Is there a difference? I mean, that was the point in the beginning, taking Ziggy Stardust's cue and combining religion and politics and saying it's really all the same. This ain't rock'n'roll, this is genocide. If you just use the inflection of your voice and say something loud at the end, like, 'Hey, what's up everyone... my DICK!' people go, 'Yesss!' It makes you consider religion as some sort of language virus.

*I understand you're in fight training at the moment. Why?*
Because I got my ass kicked the old-fashioned way at the bus stop when I was growing up. I just wanna do it because I wanna do it. It's not like I want to pick fights with people, but if I get in a fight, I get in a fight. Don't press me, because I will fuck you up.

*It's a vicious cycle, though, because if someone picks on you as a kid, then you grow up, get bigger and beat up other people – you become the bully.*
No, I didn't want to become a bully. I just didn't fight back.

*Psychologically, how has that first beat-down had an effect on your life?*
This album contains an element of revenge.

*Don't all of your records?*
No, they're more about rebellion. It's paying back but it's also paying your dues. I've earned where I've got to. I would compare this record to elements of *Mechanical Animals* and *Holy Wood* (in terms of) the feeling that I had, being in Los Angeles, and realising this is all fucked and I have to deal with it.

*Did you move to LA on the hunt for a new musical angle?*
No, I moved there thinking it was my dream. I always thought it was a special, magical place to move to. Then Columbine was kind enough to pull the rug up under me. In the midst of that

previous spread
wool coat by Givenchy by Riccardo Tisci;
latex shirt by Syren; latex gloves by House of
Harlot; nose piece Marilyn's own

this page
all clothes by Saint Laurent by Hedi Slimane;
gloves Marilyn's own

I took a moment back and I made *Holy Wood*. The first image I emerged with was me, head shaved, with all these symbols and a gun my father had given to me aged seven. He taught me how to be a sniper and brought that gun back from Vietnam. So I have accurate aim. If I wanted to be a short, 100-foot range sniper, I'd be very, very good at it. But I'm not really into shooting things.

*Guns are a recurring theme throughout your work. Does this obsession go back to your dad?*
It has to. I mean, maybe it does. It probably had a lot to do with me dealing with my mum dying while I was making the record. At the end of the day, you still die alone – spoiler alert. You die alone. It's not a depressing story. It just *is* the story. It's life.

*There's also been so much narco influence...*
Narco, narco. (*laughs*)

*...on your songs. Have you ever been on a seven-day binge?*
I don't think I've ever spent seven days on a binge. I mean, that's tough.

*What would be a typical binge for you, then?*
Three days, I guess, historically. That was probably in the era of me knowing Hunter S Thompson. He once asked me to send him the tincture of absinthe-diluted wormwood. It had a picture of a man with a dropper and an 'x' next to it, like, 'Don't put it in your mouth.' So I said to him, 'Listen up, shit eyes.' He said, 'Did you just call me shit eyes?' I didn't hear from him for a week and when I called him, I said, 'Did you get the package?' He said, 'Yeah, it didn't work.' I'm like, 'What?' And he said, 'I've been up for seven days, it didn't fucking work.'

*That's hilarious!*
Nothing good happens after three days. And nothing good happens after seven days if you have not abided by the rules of nature, which are sleep, wake up, do your job, repeat. And you know, there are definitely times when you want to expand your mind, go to different realms and go into different things, which I've done either wilfully or woefully – whichever one you want to pick – and the results have all been the same: bad.

*Sex is also central to your music. On* Mechanical Animals, *you explored alien androgyny – has there ever been a point in your life where you've felt trapped or alienated by your gender?*
You mean am I bisexual? No.

*No, trapped within your body, by the way you look.*
The very first time I got my ass kicked. I had gone to K-Mart in this yellow-and-purple basketball outfit. I went to the city kids' basketball court and they were all taller than me. I didn't get tall till I was about 18. I was around 5ft 4in (and suddenly) I became 6ft 1in. Anyway, this guy came over to me, shoved me and said, 'You're a fucking cunt.' So I went home and said, 'Mom, Dad – what's a cunt?' So that, I think, defined me at that point – not understanding the difference.

*That's when it dawned on you that you were an outsider?*
Well, I didn't understand what a 'cunt' was. The only person in my lifetime that's called me a cunt was the first person that kicked my ass. I fell and hit my head on the Tarmac. There was a bump on my head for about a week and maybe I didn't tend to it enough but eventually it evolved into something. I had to go to hospital and I found out that it was infected. They squeezed it and worms came out of my brain. I'm not even making that up. I was called a cunt, knocked down, and worms came out of my head. The end.

*Did your parents explain what the term meant?*
Their explanation was not sufficient. They just said, 'It meant that he didn't like you.' Maybe that's why I have women issues.

*Tell me about some of these women issues. You've had relationships with Traci Lords, Jenna Jameson and Stoya, and you were married to a burlesque dancer. All these women are the living embodiment of sinful fantasies. Is that what you're searching for, sexual escapism?*
Maybe. Some of the pornography I saw as a child was women having sex with animals and stuff like that. I know my grandfather would wear drag clothes underneath his clothes when he was driving a truck. My father just recently told me after my mother died that my grandfather's truck-driving gig was just a front for him selling pornography. I was like, 'Dad! My book would've been so much fucking more interesting if you'd told me that earlier!' He told me to write a new one. And he wasn't joking, either. I also did not know that (my grandfather) stashed his 60mm reels of pornography in paint cans. Which ends up being ironic, because actually my first job was painting walls. Paint was my first artistic influence, but pornography was in the paint cans.

"I would never kill myself, I'm not a quitter. If I'm going out I'm taking everyone with me, strangers first"

this page
wool coat and lace-up boots by Givenchy
by Riccardo Tisci; latex shirt, leather corset
and latex trousers by Syren; latex gloves by
House of Harlot; nose piece Marilyn's own

hair and make-up Julia Hapney; styling
assistants Virginia Fontaine, Katy Fox

*Do you think that's why you are attracted to porn actresses?*
I don't know. I think that I see something on TV, and I like it and go, 'I want that,' because I'm a child. But that's not something I saw on TV because I've never watched pornography. I've always looked at pornographic stills or pictures of women in lingerie or the Victoria's Secret catalogue, but I've never watched pornography. I can't watch moving pornography, maybe because I don't like to see other dicks. I don't know why. The three girls that you mentioned, I've never watched any of their pornography. I did not know who Jenna Jameson was and Traci Lords I knew from *Cry-Baby*. I guess it's strange, but with Stoya we were more like brother and sister.

*You've modelled for Saint Laurent and have been a muse to Gaultier. What is your view of fashion?*
The fashion world is very absurd – when you go to shows you watch people walk down the runway and you're waiting for someone to fall over, basically. It's the only reason that I've ever gone to a fashion show: to see if a girl falls over. It might sound cruel, but it is what it is. That's what everyone does, they're waiting for something bad to happen. Everyone wants to see a tragedy.

*Growing up, you were obsessed with the idea that the apocalypse was going to happen at some point. Now you've actually had 46 years on earth to get your head around the apocalypse, how would you ride it out?*
Did you just date me? Fuck you, fuck you, you fucking cunt.

*You can't call me a cunt now!*
I just did, I can. I said it.

*Now you're like the bully.*
No, I'm not. Anyway, you know what, the fashion eras I really identify with are the 20s and 30s. It was the era before people thought it was OK to wear t-shirts or sweatpants, looking like you don't give a shit. If a girl starts wearing sweatpants in a relationship, it's over. It means she doesn't give a shit any more and you're not gonna fuck her. Girls should always present themselves to you when you come home. 'Hi honey, I'm home,' and she's wearing lingerie, legs akimbo. 'Come and get it, honey.'

*Really? That's how you believe all women should act?*
My father's view of women was, 'If you wanna get a man, spread your legs. And if you wanna keep a man, shut your fucking mouth.'

*That's disgusting.*
It's foul. But that's how I was reared and raised – under the assumption that, if you want to keep a man, don't mouth off. You wanna get a man, show him your business parts. I'm not saying that's my philosophy, I'm just saying that's what my father taught me.

*Are you worried about being seen as a misogynist?*
No, I am a massage therapist. (*laughs*) I'm not sexist, but I tend to incite misogynist characteristics. I do not hate women, I love women. I just don't love what they do to me sometimes. Love is a very strange word. I love being alive. I love air. I love vodka. I love food. I love not being dead. I love making music. So when you say 'I love you' to someone, it's sort of narrow. I think if you say, 'I'm dedicated to you. I wanna be with you. You're my partner,' that's a more powerful way to express it.

*Sounds like you've had your heart broken a lot by women.*
Fuck you. (*laughs*)

*No?*
I don't know if I have a heart. I've let my guard down, I've been wounded. So if you mean heartbroken in that sense, yes. I think essentially man and woman can't function without the other, because it started that way. But it doesn't mean you're the same as I am just because we like the same movies or laugh at the same jokes. If you're in a *Bonnie and Clyde* or *Natural Born Killers*-type relationship, that doesn't mean you should expect the other person to feel the same way as you, simply because in your fucked-up mind you think you're living in a movie, which I do.

*Is your life a movie?*
I think everyone's life is a movie, it just depends on whether it's a good one.

*Your music has dissected the cadaver of pop culture for 20 years now.*
'Dissecting the cadaver of pop culture', well said.

*Thank you.*
You just wanted to put that in there.

*True. What are the results of the autopsy? Are we all fucked?*
Dead.

*Pop culture is dead?*
Dead, but zombies. That's why I will not be cremated, because I want to make sure I can come back alive. Zombies with hard-ons is something we haven't seen enough in film.

*Is that your next role?*
Well, if I die I want to die with my boots on, as they say. I also want to make sure that if I die and it's said that it was a suicide, it's false. I would never kill myself, I'm not a quitter. If I'm going out I'm taking everyone with me, strangers first.

*Phil Spector killed a woman because of his obsession with guns and sex. What's the closest you've ever come to death?*
Well I think apart from seeing other people's deaths, I've never tried to kill myself. I never try – I do. Someone says, 'You tried to kill me,' I'm like, 'No, wrong. If I'd tried I would've done it.' I don't have a death wish, I don't want to kill other people, but I will defend what I care about. I will defend what I love. I think you should be someone who stands behind their words, not someone who just says them, and that's resulted in a lot of trouble legally for me. I have put a gun in the mouth of a journalist on more than one occasion. But I was exonerated from that crime and released on a simple assault and battery charge.

*I'm glad you don't have a gun on you tonight.*
How do you know I don't?

*I'm hoping not.*
(*To assistant*) Can I have my gun, please?

The Pale Emperor is out now

# Heart Works

Björk bares her soul as never before on new album *Vulnicura*.
Here she talks to her friend, the Icelandic writer Oddný Eir,
about channelling heartbreak into powerful new creative forms

text James Merry    photography Inez and Vinoodh

In Þingvellir, Iceland, where the North American and European tectonic plates drift apart, Björk and author and philosopher Oddný Eir are discussing rifts of the human kind. There is a thick layer of snow outside the singer's house, but inside there is warmth and laughter. The pair started working together in 2008, as the Icelandic financial crisis took root. They encouraged local people to start their own 'green' startup companies as an alternative to the country's massive aluminium factories, fighting for a wider range of technological alternatives that could coexist in harmony with nature. They've shared a bond ever since, although this is the first time their conversation has been recorded or translated into English. In the conversation that follows, the pair discuss heartbreak, transformation, romantic relationships and devotion, themes that reverberate intensely through *Vulnicura*, Björk's majestic follow-up to *Biophilia* (2011). The record, which features music produced in collaboration with Arca and The Haxan Cloak, was unveiled on iTunes in January after it leaked online. A physical release will follow in March to coincide with Björk's live shows at Carnegie Hall and massive MoMA retrospective, which brings together specially commissioned new material alongside insights into her career of innovation.

BJÖRK: I was really curious, after you heard my new album for the first time last night, how you felt its themes might mirror your new book?

ODDNÝ EIR: Similar desires and challenges appear in your lyrics and in my book, for sure. It has a lot to do with trust. Devotion and trust. I really felt my last three books were nurtured by our discussions over the years. Because we haven't just been chatting about boys – well, that as well (*laughs*) – but we started at the moment of the financial crisis in Iceland and somehow I feel like we were in a personal crisis, as well. We were dealing with our relationships and we really wanted to make things right. So I made a diagram (see next page), just for fun, to visualise some of these dualities and the urge to overcome them.

BJÖRK: I think this is an amazing map. To me it's about the relationship of two people, but there are different entry points too. When I make an album, I start with desire, intuition... and then for me often the beats represent the body, and the soul is found more in the strings and the vocals. This new album, for example, is more traditional.

It's a 'singer-songwriter' kind of album, with beats and strings and heartbreak lyrics. (*laughs*) If *Biophilia* was *Star Wars,* then this album is like an Ingmar Bergman film or something; black-and-white with some violins and some angst and psychology. I was rolling my eyes like a difficult teenager when I realised it – like, 'DAMN, I'M GOING TO HAVE TO GET THE VIOLINS OUT AGAIN!' So it's almost classic, you know, so typical. But you have to just go with it and try to do it in a 21st century way which is truthful to you. Because you can't ignore that. It's part of your emotional chronology, so you have to address it and move on to the next thing.

ODDNÝ EIR: People are often afraid of conflict, because they think it will just block or break them instead of leading to something further. The miraculous thing is when both of you are looking at the relationship as a way to transform; to fine-tune what's beautiful in each other's souls.

BJÖRK: I'm so grateful when my friends or collaborators give me something to push against. Maybe you don't agree with it, but it gives you something to ricochet off. It opens an exit route. It's not about getting stuck on what's wrong, but encouraging each other to go to a new place, where it can grow. I feel that the collaborations I've been most happy with in the past have tapped into that energy. Both partners experience it as equals - they were as generous as each other and got as much in return. And you're not even counting. You give very different things, because you are very different, but somehow it's still fertile and you both grow. And if you're lucky, you can find where your mutual resistance point is, and you rub against it. Then you will be able to transform each other and show each other pathways you couldn't see before.

ODDNÝ EIR: In any relationship it can be uncertain where you are going. When you commit to the process, it's very abstract. For me it's a fertile place where everything can happen. But I've definitely met people that feel it can be frustrating, chaotic. And when one person decides that they know the way, then actually it's broken. Because they're saying that they know better than the other. So you actually have to rely on trust – that you are going somewhere that belongs to both of you, but also to nobody. (*laughs*)

BJÖRK: I actually think I'm very guided by that feeling of ecstasy when a 'merging' happens – I'm always trying to find that spot, over and over again.

I think this is probably my strength and my weakness, because most times it needs insistence to even happen. When you walk up a mountain, you don't feel good till you get to the top. That's when you get the 'bliss' moment. In both love and work relationships, it is sometimes the women – I mean not only women, but the 'feminine' in people – that expect some sort of transformation in a relationship. You show each other what you can become. And you only feel that the relationship has been successful if there has been some sort of transformation. In a way this is a feminine quality, but sometimes it gets a bad reputation, because it gets turned into, 'Oh, women, they always wanna change their man.' And for sure, when it's a dogmatic, negative thing, it's obviously terrible. But if it's done well and is liberating for everyone, then it can be a miracle. I think if we were left alone on a desert island we would lose a lot of transformational opportunities that only collaborators or friends or lovers can give to us. Or even family members.

ODDNÝ EIR: This is also what I was writing about in my new book: about the possibilities, not only of women in general, but of women getting older. There's this prejudice in our culture that the older woman is without sexual power, as she has sacrificed it. And that prejudice extends to how women's voices are perceived in art.

BJÖRK: Yeah, it's part of a bigger cliché, I think. Female musicians are expected to go fully into the emotion and then burn – to be totally consumed by it as everybody watches with their eyes and mouths open. They have to be destroyed in the end because the moral of the story has to be that letting emotion rule is bad for you. Then the patriarchy can sit and watch and say, 'That was really entertaining! But if I was to live my life like that I would die so I'm not going to do it.'

ODDNÝ EIR: Yes, there is this kind of hypocrisy in our culture. We want women to be full of emotions but then we can't handle it.

BJÖRK: Like if a woman doesn't reveal her soul she's failed in expression...

ODDNÝ EIR: Oh yes, like you've failed if you don't do it and you're second-class if you do? (*both laugh*) So you have to do it all in a different way?

BJÖRK: I made all these albums which are maybe not 'narrative' in a traditional way; they're more about the music.

And I hear people that go, 'Aww, she can't write narrative,' as if everything else is second-class music. I was playing my new album to people recently and they were like, 'Oh! Björk is back on form!' and I just wanted to stick my tongue out because it was this idea that you had to tear your heart out and just 'doof!' it on the table, like that's the only way for a woman in music to be first-class.

ODDNÝ EIR: Yeah, to say you are either completely technical and detached from emotions or you are the songwriter of the narrative, it's missing the point. I find this confusion also in literature. You told me how you feel there is this 'emotional chronology' once and my god, how I liked that term. But this chronology is often hidden from yourself. I remember you had to point this out to me, and when you described this hidden structure I saw colours floating in between the forms... Sometimes you will only feel a narrative in your subconscious. It's almost mystical. Especially in an autobiographical sense.

BJÖRK: it's exciting for me that not many women – especially musicians – have documented themselves after 40. As a kid I had Kate Bush or Joni Mitchell to look up to, because they went there and created a feminine universe all of their own. They didn't just step into a male universe as a guest, and that was really inspiring for me. And then last year Kate Bush came out after 35 years of not performing, and everybody backed her up. It was such a victory. She had been allowed to age like most male singers are allowed to. Bob Dylan can be croaky. With Johnny Cash it's charming. She still reaches all her high notes and I think it has been really inspiring for a lot of people. I actually had a magical moment during a period when I wasn't allowed to speak for three weeks, after vocal surgery. I read a Kate Bush biography and listened to all her albums in chronological order, reading the lyrics as I went. Just by chance, I was also doing a big jigsaw puzzle of a map of Iceland at the same time. As I put in the last jigsaw piece, I was listening to the last song ('Among Angels') on the last Kate Bush album (*50 Words for Snow*) and I just started crying. I couldn't work it out – if it was

from joy or sadness or both. I knew she would never have written that song when she was, like, 30. It was coarse and there was some wisdom there that you only acquire later in life. So there was this sensation of time, also having not spoken a word for three weeks, and then also looking at the puzzle with all the place names and little canyons in Iceland that I've still never been to – I suddenly realised, 'Oh my god, I always thought I would eventually go to every single one of them...'

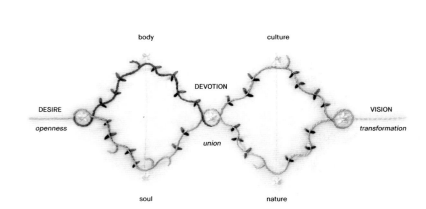

ODDNÝ EIR: I think trying to define this new territory is where our common ground is. Not only in transgressing the limits, but also in transforming what is limiting us in loving. There must be a way of being in a relationship and of being in a family.

BJÖRK: I totally believe there is a way. Maybe it comes from my punk background, this feeling that you are entering a new frontier, like the pioneer spirit. I always have to have at least one foot going into some territory that hasn't been mapped out. For my parents' generation, the way forward for women was out of the family, but I always felt that true feminism was to be able to do both – to have your job and a family. And that would be the true freedom for a woman. When I'm mapping out the cities I tour in, it has to be in flow with the family or for me it's not right. If you're just going with what works for your job or your family but not vice versa, then you're losing as a human being.

ODDNÝ EIR: Isn't it also a question of personal sacrifice in the context of some kind of sustainability?

BJÖRK: Yes, it all comes back. It's interesting how it works because love, out of all things, is probably what makes you most willing to sacrifice. Sometimes people make a sacrifice and they lose a lot from it, and other times it empowers them. In theory it would be amazing if everything was always equal, but I don't think that's how human beings function. Sometimes in the short-term you lose, but in the long-term, after some time has passed, you win. Your humility and your sacrifices have become almost saint-like, and it becomes a column of strength. We talk about people of our grandparents' generation like, 'Oh they were in a loveless marriage for 50 years and should've divorced a long time ago.' But I think in 30 years' time we will have many more people living life on their own, like brutal casualties of loneliness. Of course there are unhappy marriages that don't succeed, but I'm worried about this other development. This century – not only with family and relationships, but also with the environment and with sustainability – you have to think, 'OK, I'm not the star of the show any more." You have to work in a group, as lovers. With the new album, I sat down and was like, 'Oh my god, I have six heartbreak songs, in chronological order.' You can never plan those things. But I'd accidentally mapped out the pre- and post-heartbreak. For me as a musicologist – the David Attenborough part in me, if you will – was like 'whoa'. I had this document. That was the most interesting part of it all.

image (above left) Oddný Eir's diagram of Desire & Devotion; embroidery James Merry

Vulnicura is out on CD/vinyl on March 9
MoMA's Björk exhibition runs from March 8–June 7 in New York

"Female
musicians are
expected
to go fully into
the emotion
and then burn
– to be totally
consumed
as everybody
watches"
Björk

Her 'cosmetically enhanced' selfies hoodwinked the internet, but who is the real Amalia Ulman? The conceptual artist behind the Insta-scam of the century speaks to Trey Taylor

ome true

photography Dario Catellani    styling John Colver

How would you feel if the last picture you double-tapped on Instagram turned out to be a booby trap? You might try asking the tens of thousands of people who followed the 'fake' social media account of Amalia Ulman, a radical conceptual artist whose work examines a post-#nofilter, post-Rich Kids of Instagram world where all social is aspirational and the self is something to be performed online.

The idea of deconstructing the tyranny of smug social network bragging came to Ulman during a period of forced incapacitation. It was October 2013, and she was lying in a hospital in rural Pennsylvania after surviving a horrific Greyhound bus crash on her way from New York to Chicago, which left bones sticking out of her leg. "It was like a weird rollercoaster," says Ulman of the experience. "Up and down – my mind was trying to erase it all. But I'm very good at dealing with trauma."

Thousands of miles from her family and friends, the 24-year-old had nowhere to turn but the comforting glow of a hospital-loaned iPad. Here, in her regulation patient's gown, she began to sow the seeds of her latest project in a prescription drug-addled haze, as she Instagrammed a series of risqué selfies and snaps of her hospital-prescribed diet.

In the spring of 2014, her thoughts crystallised with the

launch of her *Excellences & Perfections project*, which she announced via a simple text-based image on Instagram stating "Part 1". Taking social media as her canvas and 'basic bitch' selfies as her muse, she reinvented herself as an aspiring actress who relocates to LA and undergoes a series of cosmetic procedures in a quest to experience life beyond the velvet rope. For four months, she fooled her growing army of followers with her counterfeit luxury lifestyle as she fanned crisp $100 bills, flashed her embellished manicures and posed at her spa-day downtime. The project climaxed with her cosmetic surgery hoax, which she termed #frankenboob. She counted down the days to her silicon gel implants in each consecutive upload. When the day finally came, she bound her breasts with the same kind of surgical tape used to treat her genuinely life-threatening wounds in hospital just a few months previously. Next she applied a flattering filter and published the discomfiting – and highly misleading – image# to her online followers.

By bringing the commitment of hardcore method acting to her art, Ulman's aspirational selfies raised serious questions of how images of beauty are used against women and how social media can manipulate our attitudes towards the female body. That might sound straightforward, but keeping 72,000 followers entertained on Instagram takes real skill. So how did she do it?

On a pit-stop in London, Ulman suggests we meet at Sheer Bliss, a budget beauty salon in a weary east London brick building. In the flesh, the artist is slight and unimposing – she can't be more than 5ft 5in. Wearing a simple beige button-down and crotcheted cardigan, she's a far cry from the babelicious vision you see online – in fact, you'd hardly notice her if you weren't paying attention. Settling back for a foot massage, Ulman explains her motivations behind her project. By exposing the gulf between image and reality, she says, her aim was to make people reflect on the artificialities and unthinking 'likes' of online social interaction. "A friend of mine told me about this girl she knows who goes to luxury hotels to take selfies because that's what goes on Facebook; that's the new capital," she says. "Better to have her selfie in an environment like that than just in her shitty bedroom." In December of last year, Ulman neatly summed up the question underlying her approach on a panel at Miami Art Basel with Instagram founder Kevin Systrom: "How do we consume things and how do they consume us?" In this simple axiom – and woven throughout her nearly-nude selfies – was hidden a plain truth: even when you show it all, you reveal very little.

The real Amalia Ulman was born in Argentina in 1989 to a Gen-X mum and tattoo artist dad, and grew up in Gijón, Spain. Most of her time was spent milling about the skate park or getting inked by her dad, until she picked up a camera. "I was secretly mesmerised by body modification when I was little," she says, sipping a cucumber water. "I grew up in a tattoo shop. My dad pierced me as well when I was younger. Mostly I was just bored, I guess. When I was growing up I was an anarchist, whereas all my friends were communists. I grew up in an expat community and was always seen as the 'other'. I was too utopian, too artistic." That artistic bent led to her first solo photography show, *Lost Between Books*, featuring a model whose face was obscured by an open book. She bagged several local art prizes and eventually chose to study at London's Central Saint Martins after Googling 'art school London'.

Ulman's work recalls that of other female artists who have gone to extreme lengths to explore perceptions of women in society. There's French artist Orlan, who underwent (for real) a series of grotesque, Picasso-like body modifications in an emphatic rejection of the pressures women face to conform to an expected standard of beauty. And there's Cindy Sherman, who wrestled back control of her body through her multi-personality, staged self-portraits, in much the same way that Ulman's work mimics unrealistic images of women the media spoon-feeds us. Through provocative, exaggerated selfies of her slinking down a dance-pole, Ulman critiques the pressures women face to achieve a dancer's bod and what it legitimately takes to get there. She's the first to admit it was a slog – twice a week for an hour and a half she worked the pole. "I had a regime," she says. "I went to the gym, pole dancing classes, got my hair and nails done – it was hours and hours of work."

Ulman has other peers, like LA artist Petra Cortright with her YouTube self-portraits, and Alexandra Marzella, better known as @artwerk6666, who keeps her online viewers lapping up crotch snaps and nipple-pinching portraits. "I think they have the same issue that I do," Ulman laughs of her friends. "Either people fall for them or feel really uncomfortable." Together, this trio are shifting their body-positive, anti-capitalist agenda closer towards their target market: generation selfie. "This is not a joke. This is very serious," Marzella told us back in July, speaking about the intent behind her seemingly tongue-in-cheek dance videos.

As Ulman's project drew to a close, some of her Instaciples caught on to the fact that something was amiss. "Is dis real? Sooooo confuzed," wrote one of her stumped followers. But she concealed her intentions to the end. She knew the project served a deeper purpose. Did she feel pangs of guilt that her following was buying in to this counterfeit dream? "Kind of – at the very end because it was so long; it was four months and it was like, 'Come on...' My aim right after I finished

the performance was to contextualise and detox and explain what was really going on." And when she did? "Most of the people who really got the performance and were attracted to it were women. They really got it. They saw the amount of work it took to build up the body while men were like, 'What? I don't get it, she just looks hot!'"

The future for Ulman is looking a little less bootylicious. She's just wrapped her first solo exhibition in New York, *Stock Images of War*, at the James Fuentes gallery. Billed as "an immersive installation exploring themes of deconstruction, confinement, fragility and war", the show presents a series of wire sculptures in a room filled with the cloying scent of baked apple strudel. But despite the real-world concerns, narcissism is never far from the surface in her work: "We need mirrors to learn our poses," she writes cryptically on her website of the exhibition.

As Ulman removes her feet from the bubbling bath, she takes another sip of her cucumber water while the nail technician starts to apply a clear gloss. It's a more natural look than she's been accustomed to lately. As her focus turns away from body image to the frontlines of warfare, perhaps it's all the armour she needs. With her gaze no longer fixed on her iPhone camera, her work is beginning to speak for itself, even as her subjects become more difficult to grasp. "I don't want to make things easy for people to understand," she says. "The point is making something good." Now that's worth a double-tap.

amaliaulman
7 months ago
#got #em #cakes
dun care bout all ur negativity #itsjustdifferent
less nervous today.... countdown

ojocondientes  isisuveuve  gliederpuppe and 232 others
like this

eddfornieles
Tap dat

esquimaux.idiom
Countdown to what?

athenaalexandrapapadopoulos
Bosom buddies! x

basedboybabinski
#bootylicious

dnlklr
Looking forward to your return

kevingrandal

vacuumnoise
I could take a better pic.

ell_svj

Leave a comment...

"Most of the people who got it were women. Men were like, 'What? I don't get it, she just looks hot!'"

Amalia wears all clothes by Dior

hair Brian Buenaventura at Management Artists; make-up Ralph Siciliano at D+V Management using M.A.C; nails Geraldine Holford at The Wall Group; photographic assistants Brian Hahn, Marion Grand; styling assistant Beatriz Maues; digital operator Andrew Lawrence; production ArtList NYC

Lucha libre ladies staged a smackdown on the Paris runway for Jean Paul Gaultier's farewell to ready-to-wear. "As I was always called 'l'enfant terrible', my wrestling name would be 'El Niño Terrible'," says the fashion provocateur. "My costume? A kilt or Breton stripe!"

# Wrestle Mania

photography Richard Burbridge    styling Robbie Spencer    make-up Yadim

all clothes and accessories by Jean Paul
Gaultier SS15

hair Tamara McNaughton at Management
+ Artists using Oribe Hair Care; make-up
Yadim at Art Partner; model Manuela Frey
at The Society Management; photographic
assistants Kim Reenberg, Enrico Brunetti,
Basil Faucher; styling assistants Victor
Cordero, Lizy Curtis; hair assistants Erin
Herschleb, Clay Nielsen; make-up assistants
Kanako Takase, Mondo Leon; digital operator
Kevin Kunstadt; casting Noah Shelley

From Destiny's Child to Sailor Moon, SS15 saw the fashion world put on its rose-tinted glasses and embrace the not-so-distant past. Susanne Madsen dusts off her bandana top and dives in

# Nostalgia, Ultra

Photography Johnny Dufort   Styling Celestine Cooney

opposite page
gingham dress by Kituzaii

this page
crochet top and lace skirt by Ryan Lo

following spread left
cotton dress by Bottega Veneta

following spread right
silk t-shirt and quilted blanket worn as skirt
by MM6

During an interview last year, Tina Knowles was asked to rate her costume back catalogue for Destiny's Child. Brilliantly serious, she declared nearly all her creations "timeless", including a symphony of red strappy tops and embroidered rhinestone denim (with the waistbands cut off for extra elegance) that the trio wore at a Hyde Park concert 15 years ago. If Ms Knowles saw the SS15 MM6 Maison Margiela show, she will no doubt have nodded approvingly when Beyoncé's red bandana top from the gig made a reappearance in industrial rubber, paired with light-wash jeans – a moment that prompted us to ask whether this season, fashion had grown Tumblr-hungry. It certainly had all of the trademark Margiela irony, and its deliberate bad taste felt like the sartorial embodiment of a #TBT accompanied by a smirking emoji and sincere red heart.

In a season where blasts from the relatively recent past are sweeping through collections, the Destiny's Child shout-out was apt. Of course, fashion has always obsessed over what *was*, forever caught in a weird maelstrom of trawling through the decades for things that will help make sense of the present and invoke the shock of the new, and its key players have long re-proposed the once-icky. But where fashion's reminiscing can sometimes feel superficial – a silhouette, a styling gimmick – SS15's neo-nostalgia feels different.

"Nostalgia sells more than sex these days," says Benjamin Kirchhoff, one half of Meadham Kirchhoff, who presented one of the most significant collections of the new season. Their emotionally raw show looked not to the 00s but instead to punk – the movement that shaped Edward Meadham's youth – in a revolt against what they see as an increasingly misogynistic, homophobic and intolerant culture. It was ultimately about proposing an alternative to the reality of today's world, and that seems to be what's driving much of fashion's current affinity for various forms of nostalgia. We want to escape into Calvin Klein's #mycalvins

reboot of its 90s logo underwear or Marques'Almeida's angsty handkerchief hemlines and low-slung miniskirts. We're revisiting a shared millennial youth, and it's both a comforting and slightly cringey exercise.

But is it too early for us to be disappearing down the millennial rabbit hole? Not according to Ryan Lo, whose hyper-girly universe centres on an adoration of things like Bridget Jones, *Sailor Moon* and *Sex and the City*. His dreamy, rainbow-hued mermaid collection channelled Carrie Bradshaw in her various guises, and was rooted in a genuine love of the show as well as a knowing wink to its cheesier qualities. "My generation still references those four women quite a lot on just about every occasion, so it's still happening and totally current. I see no difference between referencing 90s grunge and doing a *Bake Off-*inspired collection," says Lo, who came of age around the turn of the millennium. "I don't consider my work as nostalgia. I see it as reintroducing the then-cool stuff through the eyes of an Asian to the western world and putting my own girly spin on them. I guess I'm just lonely and extremely homesick!"

A return to teen obsessions lies at the heart of this season's brand of nostalgia. As Lo notes: "Adolescence is so inspiring. I like the idea of brave teenage girls. Queen Amidala from *Star Wars* was only 14 years old when she was first elected as queen of Naboo! The teenager has endless possibilities and potential." It seems there is unparalleled power and magnetism in something you desperately yearn for but can never really truly recreate – and few things have more potent magic than our adolescence.

For Faustine Steinmetz, whose debut presentation at London Fashion Week riffed on adolescent awkward-cool with its 90s-style shibori and distressed double denim, there is a "thin line between nostalgic and reactionary. What's attractive about nostalgia is not the romance, but the irony. My references to the past are there because

I like to mock it, in a way." This is what makes neo-nostalgia and millennial fashion 2.0 so intriguing: the seesaw between adoration and taking the piss. "It makes things kinkier," says Lo.

"I just can't help but disagree with everything about today's culture and values," says Steinmetz. "To me, a garment is a piece of culture. My passion for clothes has little to do with fashion." Spinning, dying and weaving all her fabrics on traditional looms, the designer's work is based on the idea of reproducing everyday, classic pieces in highly artisanal ways – another facet of the nostalgia wave. Craft holds sentiment, something that Miuccia Prada also explored this season. Backstage, she spoke of the magical powers of the artisanal after showing a collection bricolaged by more than 30 different antique brocade fabrics, which had been painstakingly reproduced.

Living in a fragmented reality where things change around us at breakneck speed, it seems fitting that we long for authenticity. There is a strong element of escapism to the season's nostalgia, which is how Dries Van Noten's SS15 hippy happening (which saw models lie down on a plush meadow-like runway) felt. It was an Instagram moment, but also an unplugged experience; a rejection of all the bad stuff that surrounds us. As Tim Blanks observed, the collection felt "critical to our mental health".

Popular consensus tends to view nostalgia as a regressive force that stops us from moving forward. The word was coined in 1688 by medical student Johannes Hofer to describe extreme homesickness, first thought of as "a neurological disease of essentially demonic cause" and later, in the 19th and 20th centuries, as a mental disorder. But as it turns out, unless you're a serious habitual worrier, nostalgia is actually mentally beneficial and can help with feelings of meaninglessness.

According to Dr Wing Yee Cheung, research fellow at the University of Southampton's school of psychology,

## "Nostalgia sells more than sex these days" Benjamin Kirchhoff

nostalgia makes you feel optimistic about the future by drawing on past feel-good moments. "It happens when people experience major life transitions, which push them to reflect on the previous stage. So, in a way, it's a growth in life," she says. This might well shed some light on why young designers like Ryan Lo are looking to the not-so-distant past for inspiration.

For many of us, our teen years will have had their share of traumatic, painful and awkward moments, but the magic of nostalgia means that we can reconstruct them with a positive ending to rewrite the narrative. In fashion, that could mean adding a witty layer of postmodern irony or applying a pair of rose-tinted glasses.

In academia, many thinkers are looking at the way we construct a false past through our obsession with reliving it, and fashion is especially fond of adding to this stylised, artificial sense of history. "Kinderwhore didn't happen," says Edward Meadham. "It was Courtney (Love)'s way of describing what she and Kat Bjelland wore, it wasn't a subculture. There weren't girls in the 90s talking about being 'kinderwhore' as there are now. They're doing it for the first time, and they're misinterpreting everything that was really happening back then. But it's natural, it's normal. We're forced to look back, because there's nothing to look *to*." Meadham's contempt for today's world led him back to his teenage "punk education", and subsequently to dream up the incredible, angry and beautiful collection that was Meadham Kirchhoff SS15, with its exquisitely worked punk pieces and feminist message that played out on a backdrop of trees strung with bloodied tampons.

"I learned about fashion via punk, via Westwood, and it was the first time I've really directly referenced that," says Meadham. "I spent six months before the show re-reading about the period, thinking how the mid-70s in England were so bleak, so brown, so conservative, and punk came from that.

I drew connections between that and the time we live in now. Everybody thinks we live in this amazing, liberal environment, which is absolutely not true. Nothing has actually improved. I think we've devolved and deluded ourselves into feeling like the world is a better place because people can assimilate. I think we should reject everything – we should get rid of this fucking shit culture we live in and create our own alternatives. The collection wasn't really about nostalgia, it was more about (getting people to) just fucking *wake up*."

"I think we look towards something we've already experienced because the alternative is celebrity culture," adds Kirchhoff. "That's what seems to be the prominent force at the moment and that's fine, it's fun – if it means something to somebody, if they can extract something positive out of it, then that's great. But I don't really know what it's actually contributing." For him, looking back to the punk era was "really to remind the world that the last time something radically different happened in culture was then." In its defiant roar, the Meadham Kirchhoff SS15 collection stirred up many of the feelings punk originally created. "The fact that this collection seems to have upset so many people when I'm referencing something that upset people 35 years ago (makes me feel like) it was a good point to make," says Meadham.

The show was also a love letter to fashion, despite what some people might think. "No one believes in fashion's power or importance any more. It's very, very depressing. I think often I've given this impression that I'm really anti-fashion. I'm so not. I *love* fashion," Meadham stresses. "But I hate that it is dead and that everybody wants it to be dead, even the people that like it most. I don't understand why in this day and age it's a dirty word to have an idea. People tell me I'm so creative, but they don't really mean it in a nice way. It's just their way of saying that what I do is hideous and unfathomable, you

know? I think it's ridiculous that there seems to be no room for anything other than homogenous shit, basically."

Whether designers are looking back in order to challenge the world we live in or reclaim their heady teenage days, it all plays into a wider search for meaning. Perhaps it's not actually bygone looks fashion wants to relive, but rather, an elusive *time*: to make an emotional connection with a lost moment, with youth. This begs the question: are we in fact becoming more nostalgic? "Maybe not our generation, but the post-internet generation, for sure," says Ryan Lo. "They have nothing which is completely new. I mean, at least our generation went from cassette tape to DVD to The Pirate Bay. Their newness is the latest iPhone model. So uninspiring."

In an interview with Dazed Digital last year, *BuzzFeed*'s Rewind editor Leonora Epstein noted how "it's not that people are more nostalgic, it's just that we have more modes of communicating", referring to the constant rehashing of yesteryear online. We're obsessed with documenting and recycling the past, turning Instagram and Tumblr into fragmented museums. In a digital age, our sense of time becomes more warped, and it gets harder for us to establish a grounded sense of the present: even last Friday is ripe for a flashback moment. It feels safe to retreat to teendom – a place that some of us never really left. "I am in so many ways the same creature I was when I was a teenager," says Meadham. "My taste hasn't really evolved. Anything which has affected me in my life came along by the time I was 17, and nothing has really interested or affected me particularly since then, not in a lasting way at least. I just feel like I've never stopped being a teenager."

"We should get rid of this shit culture and create our own alternative"
Edward Meadham

opposite page
cotton and bungee chord dress by Meadham Kirchhoff

this page
cotton dress by Viktor & Rolf

hair Kota Suizu at Caren; make-up Thomas de Kluyver at D+V Management using Chanel SS15 and Chanel Body Excellence; model Madison Stubbington at IMG; set design Georgina Pragnell at Webber Represents; photographic assistant Alex Hudson; styling assistant Poppie Clinch; make-up assistant Oonah Anderson; casting Noah Shelley

3·1 Phillip Lim

3·1 Phillip Lim

3.1 Phillip Lim

# Collections
# spring/summer 2015

photography Sean and Seng   styling Emma Wyman

Balenciaga

Dsquared2
leather shoes by Diesel Black Gold

DKNY

leather shoes by Diesel Black Gold

Miu Miu
tulle gloves by Cornelia James

Topshop Unique

Tommy Hilfiger
stockings by What Katie Did

Diesel Black Gold

tulle gloves by Cornelia James

Moschino

Fendi

hair Cyndia Harvey at Streeters using Kiehl's; make-up Petros Petrohilos at Streeters; nails Jenni Draper at Premier Hair and Makeup; model Lexi Boling at Storm; set design Emma Roach at Streeters; photographic assistants Stefan Ebelewicz, Jori Komulainen; styling assistants Samia Giobellina, Cassie Walker; set design assistants Warwick Turner-Noakes, Leslie Borg; digital operator Elliot Wilcox; production Daniel Worthington at Rosco Production; post-production Output; casting Noah Shelley

Iceberg
knickers by La Perla

# The Girl Next Door

photography Drew Jarrett    styling Robbie Spencer

Carven
earrings by Prada; socks by Trasparenze

Vivienne Westwood Gold Label
earrings by Louis Vuitton

Céline

Proenza Schouler

*earrings by Louis Vuitton*

MSGM
shoes by Converse

Givenchy by Riccardo Tisci

earrings by Prada

Saint Laurent by Hedi Slimane

fishnet tights by Fogal

Louis Vuitton

Prada

hair Naoki Komiya at Julian Watson Agency;
make-up Petros Petrohilos at Streeters;
model Olympia Campbell at VIVA London;
photographic assistants Klaus Blumenrath,
Rick Haylor; styling assistant Lizy Curtis;
make-up assistant Akari Sugino; casting
Noah Shelley

Dior

On the Verge

photography Gregory Harris   styling Katie Shillingford

Margaret Howell

Tod's
platform boots from Contemporary Wardrobe

Balmain
platform shoes from Rellik

Jean Paul Gaultier

platform boots from Contemporary Wardrobe

rag & bone

Versus Versace
platform boots from Contemporary Wardrobe

Swarovski Elements
embellished top and trousers by Peter Pilotto; embellished jacket (worn underneath) by Damir Doma; platform shoes from Reiss

Pringle of Scotland

Ralph Lauren Collection
platform boots from Contemporary Wardrobe

hair Tomo Jidai at Streeters using Oribe Hair Care; make-up Francelle at Art + Commerce; nails Holly Falcone at Kate Ryan; models Lina Berg at Fusion, Morta Kontrimaite at IMG; set design Nick des Jardins at Mary Howard; photographic assistants Stephen Wordie, Mark Luckasavage, Jake Merrill; styling assistants Isabelle Sayer, Anita Lau, Dylan Hawkinson; hair assistant Yusuke Miura; make-up assistant Mami Iizuka; set design assistants Holli Featherstone, Joe Arai, Mila Taylor-Young; digital operator Mary Gebhart; casting Noah Shelley

Maison Margiela

# Breaking the Habit

photography Casper Sejersen    styling Hannes Hetta

Hugo Boss

leather shoes by Pierre Hardy

Calvin Klein
leather sandals by Jil Sander

Isabel Marant
suede mules by Manolo Blahnik

Salvatore Ferragamo
leather and perspex shoes by Pierre Hardy

Sonia Rykiel

*leather shoes by Gianvito Rossi*

Jil Sander

Chanel
suede sandals by Haider Ackermann

Gucci
metallic shoes by Jimmy Choo

3.1 Phillip Lim
leather shoes by Pierre Hardy

Philipp Plein
suede sandals by Aquazzura

hair Cyndia Harvey at Streeters using Sebastian Professional; make-up Laura Dominique at Streeters using M.A.C.; nails Mike Pocock at Streeters; model Grace Hartzel at Next; set design David White at Streeters; photographic assistant Jakob Storm; styling assistants Josefine Forsberg, Josefine Skomars; set design assistant Alice Kirkpatrick; digital operator Frederick Heide; production Artistry London; casting Noah Shelley

# Caught in the Act

Burberry Prorsum

Dior Homme

Neil Barrett

Kenzo

Emporio Armani

Topman Design

Louis Vuitton

Comme des Garçons

Juun.J

hair Tomi Kono at Julian Watson Agency; make-up Susie Sobol; model Marc Schulze at Premier; prop stylist Eli Metcalf at Lalaland Artists; photographic assistants Matthew Hawkes, Nick Rapaz, John Burke, Billy Yuan; styling assistants Adrian Reyna, Samia Giobellina; hair assistant Sanashiro Ishigami; make-up assistant Marie Schumacher; production Ashley Herson; production assistants Devon Reitzel-Munson, Mick Ferreros; retouching BLANK; casting Noah Shelley

Paul Smith

# Stockists

| | |
|---|---|
| 3.1 PHILLIP LIM | 31philliplim.com |
| ALLSAINTS | allsaints.com |
| ALTUZARRA | altuzarra.com |
| AQUAZURRA | aquazzura.com |
| ASHLEY WILLIAMS | ashleywilliamslondon.com |
| ATSUKO KUDO | atsukokudo.com |
| AVANT TOI | avant-toi.it |
| BALENCIAGA | balenciaga.com |
| BALMAIN | balmain.com |
| BOSS | hugoboss.com |
| BOTTEGA VENETA | bottegaveneta.com |
| BURBERRY PRORSUM | burberry.com |
| CALVIN KLEIN COLLECTION | calvinklein.com |
| CARVEN | carven.fr |
| CELINE | celine.com |
| CHANEL | chanel.com |
| CHLOE | chloe.com |
| COACH | coach.com |
| COMME DES GARÇONS | comme-des-garcons.com |
| CONTEMPORARY WARDROBE | contemporarywardrobe.com |
| CORNELIA JAMES | corneliajames.com |
| COTTWEILER | cottweiler.com |
| DAMIR DOMA | damirdoma.com |
| DIESEL | diesel.com |
| DIESEL BLACK GOLD | dieselblackgold.com |
| DIOR | dior.com |
| DIOR HOMME | dior.com |
| DKNY | dkny.com |
| DONDUP | dondup.it |
| DROME | dromedesign.it |
| DSQUARED2 | dsquared2.com |
| ECKHAUS LATTA | eckhauslatta.com |
| EMPORIO ARMANI | armani.com |
| FENDI | fendi.com |
| GIANVITO ROSSI | gianvitorossi.com |
| GIVENCHY | givenchy.com |
| GUCCI | gucci.com |
| GYPSY SPORT | gypsysportny.com |
| HAIDER ACKERMANN | haiderackermann.be |
| HOUSE OF HARLOT | houseofharlot.com |
| HUSSEIN CHALAYAN | chalayan.com |
| ICEBERG | iceberg.com |
| ILARIA NISTRI | ilarianistri.com |
| ISABEL MARANT | isabelmarant.com |
| JIMMY CHOO | jimmychoo.com |
| JEAN PAUL GAULTIER | jeanpaulgaultier.com |
| JIL SANDER | jilsander.com |
| JIL SANDER NAVY | jilsandernavy.com |
| JUUN.J | juunj.com |
| J.W.ANDERSON | j-w-anderson.com |
| KENZO | kenzo.com |
| KIM WEST | kimwest.co.uk |
| LA PERLA | laperla.com |
| LOUIS VUITTON | louisvuitton.com |
| MAISON MARGIELA | maisonmartinmargiela.com |
| MANOLO BLAHNIK | manoloblahnik.com |
| MARC BY MARC JACOBS | marcjacobs.com |
| MARGARET HOWELL | margarethowell.co.uk |
| MARQUES'ALMEIDA | marquesalmeida.com |
| MEADHAM KIRCHHOFF | meadhamkirchhoff.com |
| MIU MIU | miumiu.com |
| MM6 | maisonmartinmargiela.com |
| MOSCHINO | moschino.com |
| MSGM | msgm.it |
| NEIL BARRETT | neilbarrett.com |
| PAUL SMITH | paulsmith.co.uk |
| PETER PILOTTO | peterpilotto.com |
| PHILIPP PLEIN | plein.com |
| PIERRE HARDY | pierrehardy.com |
| PRADA | prada.com |
| PRINGLE OF SCOTLAND | pringlescotland.com |
| PROENZA SCHOULER | proenzaschouler.com |
| RAF SIMONS | rafsimons.com |
| RAG & BONE | rag-bone.com |
| RALPH LAUREN COLLECTION | ralphlauren.com |
| REPLAY | replay.it/en |
| RELLIK | relliklondon.co.uk |
| RODARTE | rodarte.net |
| RYAN LO | ryanlo.co.uk |
| SAINT LAURENT | ysl.com |
| SALVATORE FERRAGAMO | ferragamo.com |
| SONIA RYKIEL | soniarykiel.com |
| STONE ISLAND | stoneisland.co.uk |
| SWAROVSKI ELEMENTS | professional.swarovski.com |
| SYREN | syrencouture.com |
| THE KOOPLES | thekooples.co.uk |
| THE NUDE LABEL | thenudelabel.com |
| TOD'S | tods.com |
| TOMMY HILFIGER | tommy.com |
| TOPMAN DESIGN | topman.com |
| TOPSHOP UNIQUE | topshop.com |
| VERSUS VERSACE | versace.com |
| VIKTOR & ROLF | viktor-rolf.com |
| VIVIENNE WESTWOOD GOLD LABEL | viviennewestwood.com |
| WHAT KATIE DID | whatkatiedid.com |
| YANG LI | yangli.eu |

# Another Man

COMING SOON

# Dane DeHaan

Photographed by Willy Vanderperre

A Crack-up at the Race Riots by Leo Gabin

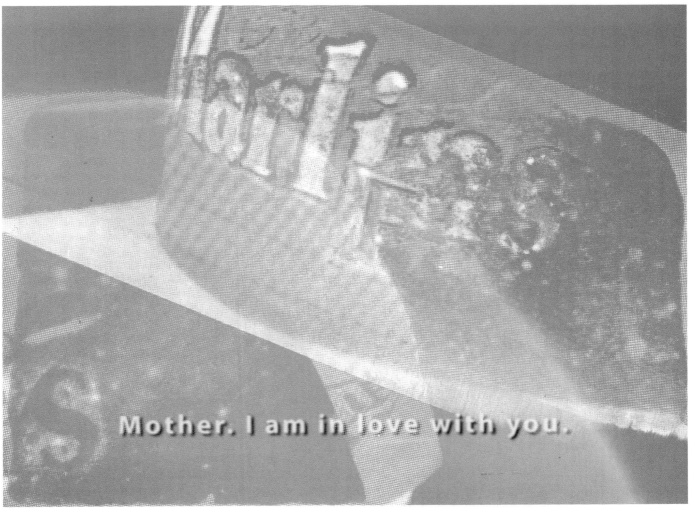

Mother. I am in love with you.

There was a f[
bald man who

14. Jodie Foster doesn't believe
in molestation

because Igor's mom had
left him in much the same way.

For our spring art residency, Belgian trio Leo Gabin – made up of Lieven Deconinck, Gaëtan Begerem and Robin De Vooght – go tripping deep into the uncanny urban terrain of the so-called Sunshine State. Inspired by Harmony Korine's 1998 novel of the same name, *A Crack-up at the Race Riots* is the group's homage to the film provocateur's literary collage. Not so much alt-lit as anti-lit, Korine's book found its way into Leo Gabin's hands in 2010, when the director gave his friends free reign to approach the work as they saw fit.

The resulting film, from which stills have been reassembled here, is as sprawling as the state it's set in. Tampa hurricanes, burning cars and body-popping baes make for a stark contrast with the Disney-fied Florida viewers may be more familiar with.

Economic stagnation weighs down everything like a swamp. "Florida is a tough state," say the artists. "It has this poetic sadness. We approached it as outsiders, looking at the state through footage on the internet, but it doesn't have to match reality or make any sense."

And why should it? Like *America's Funniest Home Videos* with added twerking, this is art for a generation that rejects sense-making in 2015 as much as it did in '98. For this collective, contemporary practice is inextricable from the way we browse the web today. "There is no better way to examine youth culture than via the self-shot imagery put online by teens." Leo Gabin's art puts a nightmarish 'no filter' hashtag on the waking teen dream.

Text Claire Healy